The Vulgate Cycle Of The Holy Grail

Arthur Edward Waite

Kessinger Publishing's Rare Reprints

Thousands of Scarce and Hard-to-Find Books on These and other Subjects!

- Americana
- Ancient Mysteries
- Animals
- Anthropology
- Architecture
- Arts
- Astrology
- Bibliographies
- Biographies & Memoirs
- Body, Mind & Spirit
- Business & Investing
- Children & Young Adult
- Collectibles
- Comparative Religions
- Crafts & Hobbies
- Earth Sciences
- Education
- Ephemera
- Fiction
- Folklore
- Geography
- Health & Diet
- History
- Hobbies & Leisure
- Humor
- Illustrated Books
- Language & Culture
- Law
- Life Sciences
- Literature
- Medicine & Pharmacy
- Metaphysical
- Music
- Mystery & Crime
- Mythology
- Natural History
- Outdoor & Nature
- Philosophy
- Poetry
- Political Science
- Science
- Psychiatry & Psychology
- Reference
- Religion & Spiritualism
- Rhetoric
- Sacred Books
- Science Fiction
- Science & Technology
- Self-Help
- Social Sciences
- Symbolism
- Theatre & Drama
- Theology
- Travel & Explorations
- War & Military
- Women
- Yoga
- *Plus Much More!*

**We kindly invite you to view our catalog list at:
http://www.kessinger.net**

THIS ARTICLE WAS EXTRACTED FROM THE BOOK:

Holy Grail: The Galahad Quest in the Arthurian Literature

BY THIS AUTHOR:

Arthur Edward Waite

ISBN 1564593452

READ MORE ABOUT THE BOOK AT OUR WEB SITE:

http://www.kessinger.net

OR ORDER THE COMPLETE
BOOK FROM YOUR FAVORITE STORE

ISBN 1564593452

BOOK V

THE VULGATE CYCLE OF THE HOLY GRAIL

THE ARGUMENT

I. THE GREAT BOOK OF THE HOLY GRAIL AND, IN THE FIRST PLACE, CONCERNING THE PROLOGUE.—The Claims and Defects of the Text regarded generally—The Secret of this Cycle—Its imputed Authorship—Its hypothetical Divisions—The Hermit of the Legend—What he Saw and Read at a Mass of the Presanctified—Disappearance of a Secret Book—The Quest of its Recovery —The Time of the Transcript thereof. II. A NEW CONSIDERATION CONCERNING THE BRANCHES OF THE CHRONICLE AND CONCERNING ITS MAJOR BRANCHES.—Divergence of the extant Manuscripts—The Incorporation of Robert de Borron Elements—The point at which their Tradition is broken, and this completely—The Arrival at Sarras—Events which lead up to the Conversion of this City—The Spiritual Palace—The Ordination of Joseph II —His Later Life—Of Evalach, the King of Sarras, who was afterwards Mordrains—Of Queen Sarracinte—Of Seraphe, who was also Nasciens— Of Celidoine, the Son of Nasciens—The Ship of Solomon—The Building of Corbenic. III. THE MINOR BRANCHES OF THE CHRONICLE.—The Later History of Joseph of Arimathæa—The Life of Petrus in Britain—Of Brons and Alain—Variations in the History of Moses—Of Simeon and his Brethren —Concerning the first Galahad—The Genealogies—Conclusion as to the GRAND SAINT GRAAL. IV. THE VULGATE MERLIN.—Its Antecedent History—Merlin as the Chief Promulgator of the Grail Mystery—The House of the Holy Vessel—Of the Second Nasciens and his History—King Pelles of Lystenoys—The Maimed King—The Daughter of the House—A Son of King Pelles—Tidings of the Grail in Britain. V. THE GREAT PROSE LANCELOT.—The Antecedents of the Story—An Undeclared Mystery of the Grail —Of Perceval in the Great Quest—Particular Grail Traditions—Missing Elements of Quest—The Genealogy of Lancelot—His Life in Faërie—Of Moses and Simeon—Of Monseigneur Gawain at Castle Corbenic—Of Lancelot and the Lady of the Bath—Elaine, the Maiden of the Grail—The Conception of Galahad. VI. A PREFACE OR INTRODUCTORY PORTION APPERTAINING TO ALL THE QUESTS.—Claims of the Questing Knights—And further concerning Gawain—A Pentagram of Chivalry—The Mystery of Divine Providence manifested in flesh. VII. THE QUEST OF THE HIGH PRINCE.—Of the Generation of Galahad—Of some things which followed thereafter—The Circumstances of his first Manifestation—Its Mystical Environment—Of the Eucharist in the Quest—Of Arch-Natural Feasting— The Quest in brief outline—The Liberation of Simeon—The Release of King Mordrains—The Voyage in the Ship of Solomon—The Term of Quest at Corbenic—The Mystery Unveiled—The Ascent of Galahad—The Doom of Earthly Knighthood. VIII. THE WELSH QUEST OF GALAHAD.—The Position of this Version—Its Variations in summary—Wanderings of the Grail—The Dolorous Stroke—Episodes of the Last Scene—Additamenta to the Vulgate Chronicles.

BOOK V

THE VULGATE CYCLE OF THE HOLY GRAIL

I

THE GREAT BOOK OF THE HOLY GRAIL AND, IN THE FIRST PLACE, CONCERNING THE PROLOGUE

THE GRAND SAINT GRAAL is the most conscious, most cumbersome, most artificial Romance in the literature. It is that also which is beyond all prodigal of wonders, and its wonders are the least convincing. In so far as concerns the History of the Sacred Vessel, it must be said that it materialises the Symbol and it distracts also the Legend. Robert de Borron finished his Metrical Romance by confessing that for want of materials he must, for the time being, hold over those branches of his Chronicle which were intended to deal with the further Adventures of Brons, Alain, Petrus and other characters of the story. In the meantime he proceeded to the Life of Merlin, bridging the gulf of centuries by a promise to retrace the path when he had obtained the necessary data, though it is possible enough that the intervening distances of time may have spelt little to his mind. All that could be construed as wanting is supplied by the GRAND SAINT GRAAL, leaving nothing undone, but working through I know not what mazes of manifold enchantment. I have said that the artifice of the design—which obtains also for its expression—stands forth in full manifestation, even upon its surface. A hand more sparing might have worked greater marvels and left some sense of realism, at least in the order of Faërie. And yet the prolix History has a certain magian touch, all paths of disillusion notwithstanding.

From whatever point of view it is approached, the text will prove otherwise to be sown with difficulties—curious things in truth of the worlds within and without; but even as difficulties these have also their occasional secret charm. There are vast sections of unnecessary matter which suggest an imperfect art of mere story-telling, while there are materials also which do not belong, more especially at their period, to the horizon confessed by that art. Moreover, nothing in reality is finished, for, as one of the sub-titles indicates, the Romance is presented as a First Branch of the Records of the Round Table, or rather it is a Prolegomenon to these. A Cycle of the literature of Chivalry is supposed to follow thereafter, which might obviously mean (1) that the author had a mind to go further or, alternatively, (2) that his intention was to establish the collated antecedents leading up to other documents which in one or another form were already in being. The second is the actual position, and in this sense there follows from the prolix introduction a great cloud of chivalrous narrative, offering herein a first point of distinction from the Trilogy ascribed to Robert de Borron. The latter lies, comparatively speaking, within a narrow compass, though it has a claim on completeness according to its own measures. There are other differences, however, which are not less marked in their character and are very much more important. The account which I propose of the memorial will differ from ordinary critical and textual apprehension by way of direct summary, since it is actuated by exclusive objects connected with the design of this study.

As the Borron Cycle of the Holy Grail is concerned with the reservation of a Secret comprised by an alleged Sacramental Formula, so there is also a Secret in the GRAND SAINT GRAAL, but it is of a different kind; and herein is a second distinction that we are called to make between the two Cycles. That particular form of Eucharistic Mystery which is veiled *ex hypothesi* by Robert de Borron and his line of anonymous successors is made void by the later Romance. As if it had planned to shew that there were no Secret Words of Consecration, an actual Mass-Formula is given in full; and although it is that of a Liturgy which is other than the Latin Rite and betrays Oriental influences, the variations are local and accidental, wearing no aspect of importance, except for Liturgical History.[1] At the same time, when the Hermit of the GRAND SAINT GRAAL is first received into that state of vision from which the transcript of the text follows, what he is promised by Christ is a revelation of the Greatest Secret of the whole wide world. That revelation is, however, a Book and one which is spoken of invariably as very small—so small indeed that it can lie in the hollow of the Hermit's hand. This notwithstanding, it is the greatest marvel that man can ever receive.[2] It was written by Christ Himself, Who committed to writing only: (1) the Book in question; (2) the Lord's Prayer; (3) the words written in the sand, according to the New Testament. To pronounce aloud the sentences contained in the Book would convulse the elemental world, and it must be read therefore with the heart.[3]

Not exactly on this consideration but not for less cogent reasons, the first thing which is apparent concerning it is that although the Hermit is covenanted to transcribe the volume and to occupy in this task the period which intervenes between the fifteenth day after Easter and the day of the Ascension; although further he states expressly that what he wrote down is that which follows his Prologue; the Secret Book committed to his charge seems obviously not that which he transmits as a memorial for those who come after him. I suppose that in registering this with a certain touch of fantastic gravity,

---

[1] Appendix I, Note 13.
[2] It is said also that the Adventures of the Grail exceed the knowledge of mortals.—Sommer's Vulgate Text, I, p. 119.
[3] *Ib.*

my motive will not be misconstrued : we are dealing with a parable or pretence, and the point is that it is not especially consistent within its own lines.[1] After making every allowance for the possible variations of late editing, both intentional and otherwise, it remains that the text of the story voids the claim of the Prologue, and this to such an extent that a substitute only is offered—so to speak—for that which was brought from Heaven for the assumed illumination of Logres.[2]

The Book of the Transcript is, by the hypothesis of the Prologue, divided into four Branches, of which the First concerns the lineage of the Hermit himself; and on the assumption that the HUTH MERLIN is correct in identifying the latter with that second Nasciens who, in the days of the Enchanter and those of Uther Pendragon, was at first of the Order of Chivalry and afterwards a Holy Recluse, it will follow that the entire Romance corresponds to this designation rather than an individual part. The Second Branch is that of the Holy Grail, which is a title of the collection itself, LI LIVRES DU SAINT GRAAL or LESTOIRE DU SAINT GRAAL, and it cannot be allocated to a section. The Third Branch is called the Beginning of Terrors, while the Fourth is the Beginning of Marvels, which in like manner will not assist towards any logical classification, as we are concerned with something that answers in all its modes and pages to the title of a Wonder-Book.[3]

The most express, most ordered, most reasoned part of the entire History is assuredly what is termed the Prologue : it is there that the Hermit accounts for the manner in which he came for a period into the possession of the alleged original text. It reads in certain passages like a story of Initiation. The *parti pris* is quick to self-deception, and one sees too easily that for which one is looking; but here are words which are exceedingly like a Sign of Recognition in some Secret Society : "The first Knight," says the Hermit, who has found refuge in a House of Chivalry, "recognised me, as he believed, by a Sign which I bore about me : he had seen me in a place which he named". But the Hermit evaded disclosures, for he was bent on concealing his mission, even as through the whole of his narrative he veils also his personality, though perhaps for the express object that it should transpire in the subsequent texts.

The circumstances under which he came to begin his story took place in Britain, 717 years after the Passion of Christ. It is to be inferred that prior to his mission he knew nothing concerning the Mystery of the Holy Grail, though he did know of his lineage, which may be intended according to the flesh or according to the mystical spirit, if its reference is to the Grades of his Initiation. On Maunday Thursday,

---

[1] One does not produce memorials for those who come after and then advise a presumed reader that they are likely to convulse the cosmos by their mere recitation; but we see that this is an affirmation of the text.

[2] I suggest that what is written in the GRAND SAINT GRAAL can be a substitute only, to save the preposterous situation created by the Hermit's claim, namely, that the text put into his hands was the work of Christ Himself. My proposal is not to be understood over seriously.

[3] See Sommer's VULGATE VERSION OF THE ARTHURIAN ROMANCES, I, pp. 5, 6.

after the office of *Tenebræ*, the Grand Master awoke him from sleep and gave him a Book to ease his doubts on the subject of the Trinity.[1] His immediate experience thereafter was the possession of a further gift, which was that of an infinity of tongues. He began reading the Book but laid it by on Good Friday, to celebrate a Mass of the Presanctified. Between the breaking of the Host over the Chalice and his reception of the Elements, he was transported to the Third Heaven, and there was enabled to understand the Trinitarian Dogma by a dilucid contemplation of the Blessed and Glorious Trinity, with its distinction of Persons combined in the Mystery of their Unity.[2] In other words, this was an ecstasy of the Eucharist consequent upon his initiation into the Sacramental Power and Grace enshrined in the Secret Book. After Mass he placed the Book in the Eucharistic Dovecote, or Tabernacle, with the intention not to reopen it till Easter Sunday, when he found that it had been abstracted strangely; and he undertook a wonderful pilgrimage in search of it.

That he might be directed rightly on his journey, the Hermit was led by an animal which combined the characteristics of the Lamb, the Dog, the Wolf and the Lion:[3] it recalls in fact that Questing Beast which appears in other Romances and, according to its figurative sense, is explained by the PERLESVAUS. Ultimately he recovered the Book, having found it reposing on the Altar in a certain fair Chapel. This restoration was followed by a vision of our Saviour, Who ordained its transcription. On Ascension Day the original was reassumed into Heaven. It will be seen that no pains are spared to exalt the work which follows this introduction : *ex hypothesi*, it is of mysterious and divine origin ; a parchment copy is produced for earthly purposes by the highest of all ordinations ; and as regards its source and nature it must take precedence of everything, even the Canonical Gospels. That which follows, however, is the extravagant story with which we are about to deal.

The Doctrine of the Trinity was the great crux and mystery which seems to have exercised the minds of those who had entered the Path of Sanctity at the period immediately preceding the literature of the Holy Grail. There was a triumph of Faith in accepting it, and he for whom it presented no difficulties had attained a very high Grade of Illumination. The Hermit of the Prologue to the GRAND SAINT GRAAL is moved profoundly by the question, and to recover a supposed memorial concerning it is that which actuates his pilgrimage in search of the vanished Book.[4] We should remember that in the year 1150 the Church had established the Festival of the Most Holy Trinity ; and it was a quarter of a century later that the Grail Legends began to manifest on the horizon of romantic literature.

[1] Sommer, *Op. cit.*, I, p. 5.
[2] The Mass is suspended by command of an Angel and so also is resumed.
[3] *Op. cit.*, pp. 9, 12.
[4] It happens to be nothing of the kind, either in fact or pretence, beyond the claim of the Prologue.

II

A NEW CONSIDERATION CONCERNING THE BRANCHES OF THE CHRONICLE

NOT the least difficulty attaching to the GRAND SAINT GRAAL, regarded as a work of "truth in the art" of its particular Mystery, is the divergence exhibited by the extant manuscripts. These differences meet us, perhaps chiefly, at the inception of the story, though they are with us even at the end. In respect of the latter there are texts that incorporate a distinct Romance which is impertinent to the design of the story. In respect of the former, it should be understood that it is of the essence of the whole design to make a beginning from the same point of departure at which Robert de Borron started his Metrical Romance; and all recensions present therefore some kind of prose version reflecting his narrative. One of them—and it is the most available of the printed texts—has only moderately grave variations from the LESSER HOLY GRAIL up to that epoch of the story when the company of Joseph of Arimathæa set out on their journey Westward; but another presents a brief summary which scarcely stands for the original. It is not part of my province to express opinions belonging to the domain of textual criticism; but I think that the design of the GRAND SAINT GRAAL is represented better and more typically by a manuscript like that which was made use of by Dr. Furnivall for the *Early English Text Society*, and this is the summarised form, than it is by a manuscript like that which Hucher selected for the first printed edition, and this is the extended version.[1]

The incorporation of Borron elements serves one purpose which is material from my own point of view, as it sets in relief the distinction *ab origine symboli* between the actuating motives of the two Cycles of literature. It will be remembered that in the Metrical Romance and its later reflections the narrative is broken rudely at that moment when the horizon has begun to expand by an inspired resolution of the Company to part into several groups and proceed Westward separately. Three divisions were involved hereby, and Robert de Borron promised to unfold their stories in due order when he obtained reports concerning them. We have seen also that the author of the GRAND SAINT GRAAL undertook to supply these missing Branches; but as the results differ, and in no light manner, from the manifest intent of Borron, it may be deduced that they are not the real history, as this might

---

[1] See F. J. Furnivall's uncompleted edition of the GRAND SAINT GRAAL turned into English verse by Henry Lovelich, *circa* 1460, pp. 1–100, in French, replacing what is missing from the Lovelich MS. Furnivall used a British Museum text in the King's Library, specified as B.R. XIV E 3. For the extended version mentioned above, see Hucher, *Op. cit.*, Vols. II, III. For present purposes I am following the edition of Sommer, VULGATE ARTHURIAN ROMANCES, Vol. I.

have been set forth by the pious minstrel. On his part there was assuredly no design to bring Joseph of Arimathæa either to the *Vaux d'Avaron* or another part of Britain. The doubtful meaning of some of his lines must be taken in connection with the general scheme, namely, to establish the Mystery of Sanctity in great seclusion under the government of a single Keeper, with a life protracted through the centuries, until the time of its possible manifestation came. The prose version, or LESSER HOLY GRAIL, is a moderately faithful transcript of his nearly complete poem, though it is doubtful regarding Joseph's final destination. The EARLY HISTORY OF MERLIN is faithful also to what remains of Borron's second Metrical Romance. Of the DIDOT-MODENA PERCEVAL we cannot speak so certainly; but in several points about which we have materials for judgment—and more especially regarding Moses—it does not correspond accurately. We have accepted indeed and enforced the almost unanimous conclusion of later scholarship, according to which the DIDOT-MODENA PERCEVAL is a speculative completion of the Trilogy, characterised by remarkable insight and the work of an unknown hand.

It must be understood therefore that the GRAND SAINT GRAAL, or the elaborate Romance which follows the parable of the Prologue, begins with a short account of the chief incidents in the Life of our Saviour and the condition of Palestine at that period. It repeats the familiar story of the LESSER HOLY GRAIL, but sometimes, as we have seen, only by way of summary, and always with many variations. The fact that Joseph is married and has a Son in his infancy at the time of the Passion of Christ may be taken as the first important point of difference. He is named after his Father, and to distinguish between them the orthography adopted by the Romance to designate the Son is Josephe or Josephes, for which in the the present account I shall substitute Joseph II.[1] The next point of difference, with which we are acquainted also, concerns the identification of the Holy Grail with the Dish of the Paschal Supper—*en quoi li fiex dieu avoit mangie*—instead of with the Eucharistic Vessel of Sacrifice;[2] but it should be said that there is another text, and this follows the description in the LESSER HOLY GRAIL. The circumstances under which the Great Palladium was discovered, after the apprehension of Christ, also vary, and in place of its abstraction by a Jew, who carries the Hallow to Pilate, it is found by Joseph himself in the House where the Pasch was eaten, and is removed by him to be kept for a memorial of the Master. As in the other Romances, it is used to collect the Blood, which, however, is done no longer on Càlvary, but in the Holy Sepulchre itself. The general lines established by Robert de Borron are followed as regards the imprisonment of Joseph, the circumstances under which he was released by Vespasian after a term of forty-two years, and the

---

[1] Sommer, *Op. cit.*, I, p. 19, containing the first reference to Joseph II. The voice of an unseen speaker tells the Father that his Son will never take a wife.
[2] *Ib.*, p. 13.

vengeance wreaked upon the Jews. All lapse of years notwithstanding, Joseph is reunited to his Wife and Son, is baptised, with a great number of his relatives, and he is directed by Christ to go with those who will follow him into distant countries, carrying neither gold nor silver, nor any material possession except the Holy Grail. It is after this point that the prototype of Robert de Borron is abandoned once and for all. The first destination—reached by way of Bethany and a certain Wood of Ambush—is the City of Sarras, situated in a country of the same name on the confines of Egypt.[1] From this land it is stated that the Saracens originated: the people are described as worshippers of the Sun, Moon and Planets. It is also this place which is termed in later Romances the Spiritual City, though it is not on account of the faith found in its citizens—who appear to have been a perverse race at the beginning and end—but because, according to the story, it contained a *Palais Esperiteus*, which name was given it by the Prophet Daniel, who inscribed it on the door thereof. The story is of course apocryphal, but the design is to shew that even the Seers of Israel were aware of the coming of the Grail, since it was in this Palace that the Eucharist was first consecrated. It was the witness on the dry land, as a certain Ship of Solomon was the witness on the open sea.

At Sarras Joseph found Evalach, its aged King, in great trouble through an invasion of his country by the Egyptians under Ptolemy.[2] Joseph commended his conversion as a certain guarantee of victory; but the King, though not disinclined, was not baptised actually until his enemies were dispersed with great slaughter. The power operating in his favour rested chiefly in a Cross painted on his shield by Joseph. The story of the war and its wonders occupies a substantial part of the narrative, and before Joseph continued his journey Westward the whole population of the country appears to have embraced Christianity. Several Churches were built in the City or its vicinity; Bishops and Priests were Ordained; and Masses were celebrated therein.

England is, however, the Promised Land which the special providence of the story has allocated to the spiritual and physical lineage of Joseph of Arimathæa; and after the departure from Sarras the sole concern of all the involved Adventures is, separately or collectively, to bring the various characters to this country and to reunite them therein, the evangelisation of the existing inhabitants being the palmary term of all. Speaking of the rank and file, apart from several of the most important personages, the good Christians are transported hither miraculously on a garment belonging to the second Joseph, but those who are imperfect come by ship. A few of the chief heroes arrive independently, under circumstances which will be described in the considerations allotted to each. Joseph of Arimathæa reaches the general bourne; and though the superior importance of his Son causes him to be almost effaced, we hear of him from time to time during long years

---

[1] *Ib.*, p. 21.   [2] Sommer, *Op. cit.*, I, p. 21 *et seq.*

of continued existence. At length he left this world to be united with Christ, unto Whom all his love was dedicated. He was buried at the Abbey of the Cross in Scotland, for which one codex substitutes Glastonbury.

There is a general sense in which the GRAND SAINT GRAAL—like the Metrical Romance of Borron—is a Book of the Divine Voice which speaks from the Sacred Vessel, though this is not used to pronounce oracles or to separate the good from the evil as it is in the earlier text. The difficulties raised by the story regarding that Mystery of Faith which it exists to shew forth are so grave and so numerous that I must be satisfied with the registration of the fact and its illustration by one instance. The whole notion of the Eucharist is changed by the supposition that, on occasion, it is administered by Angels; for on no hypothesis is Christ their Saviour or are they His Priests.

Seeing that there is no clear division of episodes in the story, so that one section can be separated definitely from another, I shall attempt only a general grouping. The Master-Branch of the whole prodigal Romance is that which embraces the mission of Joseph II: this is of the essence, and all else is, in comparison, of an accidental order. About his central figure the wonder of the Grail converges and the confused cloud of marvellous incidents: from the first even to the last, he is thus steeped in a Light of Mystery that "never was on land or sea." Prior to the arrival at Sarras a command was received from the Son of God to build an Ark,[1] similar to that of the Old Covenant, for the reception of the Holy Vessel. Public devotions were to take place before it; but only Joseph and his Son had a right to open the Shrine, to look into the Reliquary and to take it in their hands. Two chosen men were deputed to carry the Ark on their shoulders when the Company was on the march. The design was evidently to invest the new symbol with the same authority as that Palladium which once belonged to Israel. To provide sustenance for the band during their travellings, each disciple—after the Daily Service of Prayer—found in his lodging the food which he desired in abundance; but it is not said that this sustenance was provided by the Holy Grail.

While the conversion of the King and the issue of the war were pending still at Sarras, things of far other importance were taking place in respect of the Sacramental Mystery under the charge of Joseph and his Son. The Pilgrims had been lodged on their advent in that building which was named the Spiritual Palace. The inhabitants of Sarras did not know why it had received this designation; but the arrival of the Christian Cohort was to reveal the Prophetic Mystery—firstly, by the presence of the Ark and the Grail therein and, secondly, by the sacred marvels which accompanied the Ordination of Joseph II, with Christ manifested visibly as the Celebrant-in-Chief.[2] In that Palace, on the day following their arrival, the Holy Spirit advised Joseph the Father that his Son had been chosen to guard the Grail, as

---

[1] Sommer, *Op. cit.*, I, pp. 20, 21. [2] Sommer, *Op. cit.*, I, pp. 31–41.

the Aaron of the new Rite; that he was to be Ordained by the Highest Consecration and must transmit the Priesthood to those whom he deemed worthy. Joseph II received also the power of handing on the Sacred Vessel to whomsoever he would. It is as if Christ said to his successor: "My peace I leave with you; My peace I give unto you".

When the Company were worshipping before the Ark in the Spiritual Palace, the Holy Spirit descended in still fire, as at another Pentecost, and entered into the mouth of each one of them, like the Eucharist of some final dispensation which has not been declared on earth. It communicated, however, a Gift of Silence instead of the Gift of Tongues. A Voice spoke also and though apparently it was that of the Spirit, it was also the Voice of Christ. The discourse was memorable enough; but I can speak only of its end, when the younger Joseph was directed to approach and receive the most great honours which could be conferred on earthly creature. He opened the door of the Ark and beheld a Man clothed in a terrible vestment of scarlet flame. There were also five Angels apparelled after the same manner, each having six wings of fire, recalling the four of Ezekiel. In their right hands they held various symbols of the Passion—about which we have heard already—and each in his left carried an ensanguined sword. The human figure was that of Christ, with the five wounds upon Him. It is said by the text that the Ark had been magnified strangely, so that it could hold the Divine Personalities of the vision: but I conclude rather that when the door was opened, those who were empowered to behold looked as into a seering-glass, which contains at need the earths of the universe and the earths of the starry heavens, with all that dwell thereon. The state of the Second Joseph is shewn by the words addressed to his Father, praying that he should touch him in nowise, lest the speaker be drawn from the joy of his entrancement. That which he beheld next was the Crucifixion itself, presented in Ritual form, with the Angels for actors therein. It seemed even as in one of the Greater Mysteries which I have seen with my own eyes, when the Adept Master is set on a Cross of Dedication and the Officers of the High Ceremonial are those who combine to immolate him. But the design in the case under notice was rather to certify concerning the Vessel of the Grail, for the side of Christ was pierced and the *sang réal* poured therein. The scene closed and a new scene was opened, this time more especially before the eyes of Joseph the Father. That which he beheld was an Altar, within the Ark, draped in white over red, bearing the Sacred Dish, the Nails of Transfixion and the ensanguined head of the Lance. These objects were arranged on the Epistle and Gospel sides, but in the centre—or Place of Consecration—and covered with a white corporal, there was a Rich Golden Vessel with covercle, also of gold, and it is recorded that all precautions were taken that the contents should remain hidden. A Procession of Angels entered with lights, aspergillus, thurible, incense-boat and then—but not in all texts—one carrying a Head, as I suppose, on a salver, and another with a Drawn Sword. This Pageant went about the House, for a Rite of High Consecration, the Grail being also carried, and Christ entered, even as the Priest of the Rite, clad in Sacramental Robes for the Celebration of Mass. The Circumambulation being finished, for the cleansing of the whole place—which, in spite of its name, had been the abode of evil and the spirit thereof—Christ told Joseph II that he was to receive the Eucharist and, as if constituted a Secret Pope, that he was made and Ordained, Sovereign Bishop, reigning over the World of Christendom.[1] He was clothed with rich Episcopal Vestments and set in an Episcopal Chair, which the text says was still preserved at Sarras, where it proved to be another Siege Perilous, for whosoever sat therein was maimed or destroyed utterly. Joseph was anointed by Christ, and with the oil which was used for this purpose the Kings of England were hallowed in later years up to the time of Uther Pendragon; but it was missing at his coronation. The Ring of Investiture, given to the new Prelate, thus enthroned strangely, could be counterfeited by no human skill, nor could words express the virtues contained in its jewel.

When the Ceremony was at length over and the Divine Discourse had explained one by one the spiritual significance of each part of his clothing, Joseph II was instructed by Christ to Consecrate the Elements, and it came about thus that the people of the new exodus communicated for the first time: but the Host which was elevated by Joseph was the body of a child and that which was received by the faithful, in the mouth of each one among them, was living and undivided flesh. The administration to the cohort of worshippers was performed, however, by Angels; one of whom took the Paten together with the Chalice and placed both of them in the Holy Vessel of the Grail.[2] Whether the Precious Blood adhered to the Eucharistic Vessel and the content of the Reliquary thus suffered diminution we do not know, nor the purpose otherwise of the Ceremony, which, fortunately for the spiritual side of *la haute convenance*, is not repeated either in the Romance itself or anywhere in the literature.

Thus was the Second Joseph Consecrated in the Super-Apostolical Degree, and thus did he see—at least in the sense of the story—all Christ's Mysteries openly. The issues which are raised by the narrative are much more complicated than will be gathered from the preceding summary. Scholarship has paid little heed to the importance of the Sacramental Question and all connected therewith; but it has not overlooked entirely the Pontifical Supremacy which is ascribed to the reputed founder of Christianity in Britain. While the ecclesiastical consequence to these islands is perhaps the only thing which can be

---

[1] According to the remarkable words put into the mouth of Christ, the Second Joseph became the *nouvel evesque de ma crestienté nouvele*—as if an older Christianity were about to be supplanted. The real meaning is that Christianity was new in the world.

[2] Sommer, *Op. cit.*, I, pp. 40, 41. This is the kind of Transubstantiation: it is perhaps more likely to have been denounced than approved by the Council which met at Lateran in 1215 for the formulation of the Dogma, supposing that it had been brought forward. It should not be inferred that communicants received in both kinds.

said to stand forth clearly, it must be added that if the intention was to make void one claim of the Papacy, there was never a design so clouded and veiled so sedulously. The Brief for any Secret Pontificate is proclaimed much less openly than the general brief for the Official Church, with all its ways and laws, as we are acquainted with its body —politic and spiritual—at the period. Still it is said expressly, in words ascribed to the Master: (1) that Joseph has been chosen as the first pastor of a new flock; (2) that his eminence is comparable explicitly in the New Law with that of Moses, the Leader of Israel, in the Law which now had been superseded; (3) that wherever he went, converting people and places, he was there to consecrate Bishops and ordain Priests, who would have power to bind and loose, even as the Apostles;[1] and that, in fine (4), to the Younger Joseph was committed the government of souls but to the elder that of bodies—the spiritual and temporal powers. It does not appear especially that the latter ever exercised his prerogative; but it may be recalled that whereas the first issue of the temporal power was after the spiritual kind, the second was after the political—on the one hand, Joseph II, who never married, whose Office was devised by election; on the other, Galahad le Fort, a later Son of the original Joseph, who became an earthly King, who was anointed with the mystic oils by his Brother and who reigned gloriously.[2] We may speculate, though it will be all in vain, as to what was in the mind of the author when he substituted an elder Son for the Father and, as if further to confuse the issues, gave both of them the same name. Whatever the explanation may be, from that moment when the younger man assumed the reins of government in the spiritual degree, the older ceased to retain even the shadow of power. As regards Galahad le Fort, his birth took place in Britain, and it was foretold to his Brother in a vision that he would be the ancestor of a holy lineage of many men of religion, who should maintain the Name of our Saviour in all honour and all power throughout these islands.[3]

His great election and his association in the highest notwithstanding, the Second Joseph was not intended to escape without the purgation of suffering. When he and his Company were at Orcauz, in the district of Sarras, he was punished for attempting to bind a devil who was hovering over the dead bodies of certain Saracens: for this indiscretion, a Great Vindicating Angel, with a marvellous countenance, drove a spear into his thighs and left the weapon therein. Subsequently, he was healed by another Angel, who drew out the head of the spear. That which Joseph II should have effected was apparently the conversion of the heathen and having failed in this he was not to

---

[1] At the beginning of his Pontificate he is said to have Consecrated thirty-three Bishops—a considerable number under all the circumstances; but unfortunately we hear nothing further concerning them.

[2] *Op. cit.*, p. 282. An example of the Church creating and investing Kings.

[3] Here is a note of intention, the fulfilment of which is wanted. The said Galahad becomes King of Hocelise-Gales or Wales, and founds an Abbey. Among his descendants were Urien, Iwain and above all the true Galahad—the Son of Lancelot and last Grail King. Of the "many men of religion" we hear no more in the Vulgate Cycle.

intervene between the destroyer and the victims. I mention these matters, firstly, because the office of wounding in the thighs recurs so continually in the romances, and, secondly, to note that for some obscure reason the injury in question never befalls the Questing Knights. The Lance used on this occasion is also important because of its after-history, for it was destined to prove the beginning of those great marvels which would occur in the land of Britain. At that time it is said that the Lance will drop blood and will strike—also in both thighs—another personage of the Mystery, a Knight full of charity and chastity, who will suffer for as many years as Joseph had carried the weapon in his own wound for days.[1] These, on the computation of the victim, proved to be twenty-two. The reference is here to King Pellehan, whose wounding is narrated, as we shall find, in the HUTH MERLIN, and who is healed in the QUEST OF GALAHAD: the wounding in question is the Dolorous Stroke inflicted by the poor Knight Balyn; and it follows that the GRAND SAINT GRAAL gives an origin of the Lance-Hallow which either differs from that of all other texts or it has omitted to mention that the Angel of the Judgment used the Spear of the Passion.

When the Company of Pilgrims at length reached the sea-shore, from which they must cross over to Britain, those who bore the Ark of the Grail on their shoulders walked over the intervening waters as if upon dry land: of the others, those who were in a state of grace crossed on the shirt of the Second Joseph, as if on a raft; but the evil livers were left to fare as they might till ships could be found to carry them. I am not concerned with the events which followed the arrival of all and sundry in the promised land of their inheritance; but as regards Joseph II, his evangelical journeys through England, Scotland, Wales, Ireland and, as it is said, other strange countries, continue through the rest of the narrative, till at last he visits King Evalach in an abbey which had been founded by the latter and informs him of his own immediate death on the following day.[2] This occurred accordingly at the Hour of Prime next morning, and he was buried in the Abbey. So was Joseph II gathered into the Kingdom of the Father;[3] and I pass now to the history of one who was designed as a witness through the centuries to that Mystery which was from the beginning of Christian Times and who could enter into his rest only in the arms of Galahad—the High Prince who was to come in the days of Quest.

King Evalach received the name of Mordrains in Baptism, and he remained in his Kingdom after Joseph and his Company continued their journey Westward. The design of the story, as we have seen, is, however, to bring all its characters into *la bloie Bretagne;* and with this object it puts the most complicated machinery to work for some of the

[1] Sommer, *Op. cit.*, I, pp. 77–81.
[2] *Ib.*, p. 284.
[3] The dying Pontiff invested Alain, the Son of Brons, with the Holy Grail, p. 286.

THE VULGATE CYCLE OF THE HOLY GRAIL 183

chief heroes. I must speak only concerning the term and its attainment, omitting in the present case the visions and bodily transportations which befell Mordrains for his further instruction and purgation. He left Sarras ultimately and for ever, taking his wife with him and three hundred barons, and proceeding to the rescue of Joseph, who—as a revelation told him—was imprisoned by the King of North Wales. His own realm was committed to the charge of the good Knight Aganore, who was to be King in his place, and so to remain if he did not return himself. He carried with him the White Shield by the help of which he overcame the powers of Egypt, so that this passed also into the West and was kept in perpetuity as one of the Lesser Hallows. The journey took place by ship in the ordinary way; Joseph and his people were rescued in due course; and of all their enemies not one was left alive. For this providence public thanksgivings took place in the presence of the Grail, the Ark of that New Covenant being set open for the purpose. Evalach, who had experienced already the delicious effects which followed an Exposition of the Sacred Vessel, desired to see with his own eyes the interior of the Sanctuary from which the Grace appeared to emanate. Though incapacitated by wounds received in the recent combats, he went to the door of the Ark and he saw the Holy Dish and the Chalice used for Eucharistic purposes. He saw also Bishop Joseph clothed in those beautiful vestments in which he had been consecrated by Christ. The Romance says that no mind could conceive and much less any tongue express all that was discovered to him. So far, he had been kneeling with head and shoulders bent forward, but he arose now and pressed nearer. In vain a voice issued from a burning cloud and warned him to desist: he advanced his head further, when paralysis and blindness overtook him. Of all his members he preserved only the use of his tongue, and the first words which he pronounced were those of adoration, even for the misfortune which had befallen him and which he recognised also that he deserved for surprising Divine Secrets. At the price of his health, and of age-long suffering thereafter, he would not have renounced the knowledge which he had attained in the Ark.[1] One of the spectators asked what he had seen, and he answered: "The end of the world, the Marvel of all marvels, the Wisdom which is above wisdom, the King of every king." The last wish recorded on the part of Evalach, who henceforth was to be termed Mehaigné—that is to say, the Maimed King—was that he should be carried to a certain Hermitage far from other habitation, as the world and he had no further need for one another. The second Joseph approved, because the day of Evalach's death would not be witnessed even by his children's children. He was taken on a litter to the Hermitage and placed before an Altar—presumably in a Chapel thereof—where he would be in the presence of the Body of the Lord whenever Mass was celebrated. Upon the site of the Hermitage a fair Abbey was built subsequently, and there

[1] Sommer, *Op. cit.*, I, pp. 241-243.

Mehaigné remained till the coming of the younger Galahad—or, as the chronology of the story states, for 200 years. On the day which preceded the death of Joseph II that First Bishop of Christendom anointed the King's White Shield with his own blood, thus making a second Cross upon it. It was reserved for the High Prince Galahad, and should anyone attempt to use it in the meantime he would repent it quickly. Mehaigné regained his sight so that he could behold this Shield and the Ceremony of the Unspotted Sacrifice.

With the story of Evalach there is connected that of his wife, Queen Sarracinte. While her husband was in warfare with the hosts descended from Egypt, she sent for Joseph to ask news concerning him, praying the Apostle to intercede with God that He would turn him to her own belief. Her mother had been converted through the offices of a certain Hermit, and this, assisted by a vision, caused her to be Christened herself. Thereafter she was permitted to see a white box which was kept by the elder lady among treasures of jewels; and this on being opened proved to contain the Christ under the Element of Bread. The mother took the Host in her presence, for she was departing this life. She charged her daughter to keep the box secretly, in the hope that she also might have Christ in her company. When the mother was dead, Queen Sarracinte went to the hermit and obtained from him another Consecrated Host, as a Sacred Treasure, keeping it in the same Tabernacle and performing her devotions in its presence.[1] Outside this amazing Reservation, the point of importance is that although Joseph II was, by the hypothesis of the story, the first Priest to Consecrate the Elements of the Eucharist, this was being done already—apparently long before—by a Hermit in Sarras, who must have derived from the ordinary Apostles. There is a suggestion of strange implicits in the names of the next character which is placed on my list for inclusion in these major branches. He was Seraphe, in his days, as a paynim, carrying an axe keen as a serpent of fire and evoking at his need the vision of a White Knight mounted on a White Horse and dealing arch-natural destruction. In Baptism, with the others who elected to be redeemed out of Sarras, he assumed the name of Nasciens, as if in a new generation he had been received into the *militia crucifera evangelica*, with a mission to enter the West and preach the Gospel with his sword. Seraphe was the Son-in-law of Evalach the King—a large man, strong-boned and broad-shouldered. Great and many were the miracles which brought him by slow stages to the Isles of Britain; but I will speak only of his sojourn on the Turning Island, from which he was rescued by that Mystical Ship of Solomon which fills so important an office in the QUEST OF GALAHAD.

Nasciens watched the Vessel coming to him fast over the sea: it was "richer" than any other in the world, but no one was visible therein.[2] He prepared to go on board, when he saw golden letters in the Chaldaic tongue giving warning that those who entered must be

---

[1] Sommer, *Op. cit.*, I, pp. 70, 71.   [2] Sommer, *Op. cit.*, I, pp. 120–137.

THE VULGATE CYCLE OF THE HOLY GRAIL 185

full of faith and clean in every respect. He was deterred at first but after fervent prayer he entered, believing that the strange Ship had been sent by God. He found therein a Mysterious Couch, having at its head a Crown of Gold and at the foot a marvellous Sword, which was drawn ten inches out of the scabbard. Connected with the Bed there were three Spindles of strange colourings, though not as the result of artificial tincture: one was red, another white and the third green. The story of the Ship is recounted at great length, but to summarise it shortly, the Royal Prophet of Israel had learned by a Message from Heaven that the last Knight of his lineage would exceed all other Chivalry as the Sun outshines the Moon. By the sage counsel of his wife, Solomon built this Ship so that it should endure for 4000 years, with the double object of making known to Galahad not only the royalty of his descent but the fact that the Wise King was aware of his predestined birth in a due time to come. The building was accomplished in six months, and then the Queen told him to provide King David's Sword as an arm of might for his descendant. It was adorned with a new handle, pommel and sheath—all of great virtues—and a writing about it said that no man should draw it with impunity, save one who passed all others in prowess and perfection of virtue. Solomon would have provided rich hangings also, but was deterred by his wife, who testified that they must be foul and of her own making, till another woman should, in the coming time, substitute draperies that were glorious. The High Office was reserved therefore for the most fair, faithful and unearthly Sister of Perceval. In this connection, I may say that one of the side-problems of the whole narrative is that in spite of the wonderful counsel which Solomon receives from his wife, and in spite of the sacred, exalted meaning attached to the Ship which was built by her directions, she is described as a woman who had deceived him and had embittered him regarding her sex.

The wooden bed seen by Nasciens was placed also in the Ship, and the Sword was laid thereon as well as the Crown, which was also that of David. By the same unaccountable directions the three Spindles were of wood derived from the Tree of Knowledge in the manner here following. Adam and Eve ate the forbidden fruit; the apple which she gathered brought with it a branch; the fruit was separated by Adam and the branch remained with Eve, who preserved it in their exile as a memorial of her misfortune. It was planted by her and became a great tree, which—both within and without—was white as snow. One day, when they were seated beneath it lamenting their unfortunate condition, Eve called it the Tree of Death; but a voice bade them comfort one another, for life was much nearer than death—whereupon they termed it by substitution the Tree of Life. They planted cuttings thereof, which grew and flourished: these were white like the parent tree, but after the conception of Abel they turned green, bearing flowers and fruit. It was under the first tree that Abel was murdered—when it changed from green to red and no longer bore flowers or fruit: in later times it was called the Tree of Counsel and of Comfort.

When the Ship was garnished fully Solomon placed a letter beneath the Crown, giving warning to his descendant against the wiles of women and asking to be held in his remembrance: he recounted also the building. The Ship was launched; the King saw in a vision how a great Company of Angels descended and entered therein, as it sailed far out of sight.

Nasciens learned further that the Ship typified the Holy Church of Christ; and as the latter has only faith and truth therein, so in its symbol no faithless men could have part: confession and repentance were necessary qualifications to enter Church or Ship.[1] The inscriptions in the Vessel were Holy Scripture: in a word, as the text suggested, it was a Symbol rather than a Ship. The sea over which it sailed signified the world; the bed was the Holy Altar, on which the Divine Son is consecrated and offered daily: in another sense, it was also the Cross of Christ. The white spindle meant Christ's virginity, the red one His humility and love, while the green one signified His patience.

So far as regards the Ship of Solomon; and in respect of Nasciens himself, before closing his story, I must speak of two visitations which befell him. Soon after his conversion he was filled with the same desire to know the Mysteries of the Grail for which Mordrains paid afterwards so heavily and yet was recompensed so well. He raised up the Paten which covered the Sacred Vessel and by his own account he beheld the foundations of knowledge and religion, the beginning of all bounty and all gentility.[2] We may remember here the old poet who said that Christ was "The first true gentleman that ever breathed"; and doubtless the Sacramental Mystery is also a Mystery of Courtesy. Nasciens was blinded for his presumption and remained in this affliction till the healing of Joseph II from the wounding of the Angel. His second visitation occurred on board the Ship of Solomon, wherein he had been united with his Son and subsequently with King Mordrains. To the latter he shewed the Sword of David; but when the King took it in his hands the weapon broke in two pieces and rejoined as suddenly. At this moment they were warned to leave the Ship, and in the act of obeying Nasciens was wounded grievously between the shoulders by the Sword.[3] He regarded this as a chastisement in loving-kindness for his sins; but the episode is made more intelligible by another codex, which shews that he was tempted to draw the Sword from its sheath and use it as his defence against a giant when no other weapon was available.[4] It broke in the mere brandishing and so remained till it was rejoined, unaccountably enough, by the handling of Mordrains. The wounding follows also in this case. Towards the close of the story a certain King Barlans finds the Sword

---

[1] Sommer, *Op. cit.*, I, p. 139.
[2] *Ib.*, pp. 79, 80. It was therefore no Dish but a Chalice. It is said otherwise that Nasciens saw the wonder of all wonders—that is, God the Almighty.
[3] Furnivall's text of Lovelich, p. 470.   [4] Sommer, *Op. cit.*, I, pp. 161-163.

THE VULGATE CYCLE OF THE HOLY GRAIL

of David in the Ship of Solomon and uses it to slay Lambor, who was one of the twelve sons of Brons and at that time Keeper of the Grail. There followed great sorrow and suffering in the lands of both rulers; both were ruined by the stroke, and Barlans, on restoring the weapon to the Ship and sheathing it therein, fell down dead. It will be seen that a kind of Enchantment thus befalls these parts of Britain, though the GRAND SAINT GRAAL is rather the Cycle of Adventures than that of Enchantments. The Sword was to remain sheathed until drawn by a Maiden—that is to say, by the Sister of Perceval.

There is another tale of a Sword which belongs properly to a different branch of the Romance; but it may be mentioned in this place. Joseph of Arimathæa is wounded, as usual, in the thigh by a false steward, leaving half of the sword in the wound. With the upper half Joseph heals a Saracen Knight, whom he has converted newly, and then uses it to withdraw the point from his own flesh: it comes out unstained by blood, and Joseph foretells that the two parts shall not be joined together till he arrives who shall end the Adventures of the Grail. This is the Hallow which is resoldered by Galahad at Corbenic when the Holy Quest has ended.

So far as Nasciens is concerned the remainder of the story deals more especially with his deeds of valour in connection with the conversion of Britain, which he reached at length by ship and was instrumental in bringing over those who had been left on the further shore by reason of their lapse from grace. His death took place prior to that of the Second Joseph, and he was buried in the abbey of white monks where Mordrains awaited his end.

Celidoine, a son of Nasciens, is in one sense a lesser character, but in the symbolism of the story he seems to stand for something that is important. He is said to have been born under the happiest of starry influences and was himself a reader of the stars,[1] from which he drew presages and on one occasion insured a Christian victory in consequence. The meaning of his name itself is explained to be the Gift of Heaven. One day Mordrains had a vision concerning him, and therein he was represented by a lake, into which Christ came and washed His hands and feet. This signified that God visited Celidoine daily because of his good thoughts and actions. Nine streams issued from the lake, typifying the boy's descendants. Into eight of them Christ passed also and made a similar lustration. Now the ninth was troubled at the beginning—foul even and turbulent—but in the middle it was translucent as a jewel and at the mouth more sweet and pleasant than thought can picture. Before entering this stream Christ laid aside all His vestments and was immersed wholly—that is to say, in the good works of Galahad. The troubled source signified the stain on that Knight by reason of his conception, and the removal of the vestments meant that Christ would discover to the *haut prince* all his Mysteries, permitting him in fine to penetrate the entire Secrets of the Grail.

[1] Sommer, *Op. cit.*, I, pp. 291, 293.

The external life of Celidoine, who reached Britain by himself in a boat, does not concern us except in broadest outline. As his father wrought with the Sword of earthly Knighthood in the cause of Christ, so did the son fight with the Sword of the Spirit—that is to say, with the tongue of eloquence, and paynim clerks and sages could not withstand him. Among many others he converted the Persian King Label and was married to his daughter. As he was a prodigy from the beginning and was knighted in his eighth year, he is comparable to a more sainted Merlin.

One section of the Romance which calls to be included among the major branches, and may be considered by some as most important of all, has been reserved here till the last; and this is the permanent House of the Holy Grail. During the Keepership of Joseph II the Vessel and the Ark which contained it shared in the travels of the Apostolate; but it found a place of rest during the reign of his Successor, who was Alain, as we shall learn later. With a hundred Companions he had proceeded to *Terre Foraine*, where the King was a Knight of worth but a paynim and also a leper.[1] He inquired whence his visitors came and was told, from Jerusalem. He asked further whether his disease could be cured and was informed that this was more than possible if he forsook the Evil Law and became a Christian. Hereunto the King consented and after his Baptism he was healed by the sight of the Grail, this being the only occasion on which the Sacred Vessel was shewn to a stranger. It is important also to note that though Alain was Keeper of the Hallows he was not an Ordained Priest and employed one for the purpose of baptising. It follows therefore that the Episcopal Functions of Joseph II did not devolve on his Successor, while it is certain also that there was no sacerdotal character attributed to still later Wardens and, among others, to King Pelles, who was Keeper in the days of Galahad. The new convert was Christened Alphasan, and he proposed to build a Castle for the reception of the Grail, to marry his daughter to Joshua, a brother of Alain, and to make him the heir of his kingdom if the Grail remained therein. Hereto Alain consented: the Castle was built; and at its completion they found an instruction emblazoned in red letters on one of the gates, saying that it should be called Corbenic, the meaning of which, as we know, is the Treasury of the Holy Vessel.[2] This is on the authority of the text and it is not an unreasonable persuasion to believe that the author knew what he intended to convey by a word which he seems to have compounded; but as it has not given universal satisfaction we have variants, of which some are as follows: Carbonek=Caer Banawc —the Castle of the Corners, or the Square Castle, but this has nothing to commend it; Corbenic=*De Corpore Benedicto*, which is high phantasy, but is convincing in that sense; Cor-arbenig=the Sovereign Chair, which is perfect past all desiring if the House of the Grail was the seat of a Secret Doctrine.

[1] Sommer, *Op. cit.*, I, p. 286 *et seq.* [2] Furnivall, *Op. cit.*, pp. 331, 332.

The Holy Vessel was placed in a fair chamber, as if on an Altar of Repose; and on the next Sunday Joshua was married to the King's Daughter. His coronation also took place, and in the feast which followed the Company was replenished by the grace of the Grail with all manner of delicacies. That same night the King made the fatal mistake of sleeping in the palace which he had built, and he awakened to witness a Mass of the Grail, celebrated in his room apparently. It was, I suppose, at the term of the Service that the Vessel is said to have been removed suddenly, and there appeared one wearing the likeness of humanity but composed as if it were of flame. He upbraided the King for reposing in a House so holy as that where the Vessel was worshipped; and as a warning to all who should come after he smote him through both thighs with a Sword. The Sword was withdrawn, the figure vanished, and Alphasan died ten days afterwards. It was in this way, and at first by the voice of the victim, that Corbenic came to be called the Palace of Adventure:[1] many knights attempted to sleep therein subsequently; but they were always found dead in the morning, one strong hero of Arthur's Chivalry excepted, and he suffered for it otherwise.[2]

III

THE MINOR BRANCHES OF THE CHRONICLE

THE things which remain over for consideration at the term of this inquest are chiefly derivatives from the Metrical Romance of Robert de Borron, including those further Adventures and Histories which he promised to provide if he could. It was not sufficient for the unknown author that England was the Spiritual Patrimony guaranteed to the Eldest Son of the new Church of Christ and the first Bishop of Christendom: that he might exalt it further, he transferred thereto several episodes which had been allocated in the work of his precursor to regions on the hither side of Syria, or wherever he brought the Company of Joseph to its first prolonged halt. The most important of these postponements is the doom which befell Moses: it is told also differently and is connected with a collateral story concerning one who was fated to suffer a similar punishment, of which the Lesser Chronicles know nothing. This personage is Simeon, who is said to be the father of Moses and is first referred to when the Company are crossing the Channel on their way to Britain. Simeon and his son sink then into the water because they have broken their vows of continence, and they have to be saved by the others.[3] Long after the arrival of the whole Fellowship at the term of their voyaging we hear first of

---

[1] Sommer, *Op. cit.*, I, p. 289.   [2] The reference is to Monseigneur Gawain.
[3] LESTOIRE DEL SAINT GRAAL in Sommer's VULGATE ARTHURIAN ROMANCES, I, 211.

the Grail Table, at which Joseph II and Brons sit together, with a wide space between them; but the explanation of the Empty Seat differs from that of Borron, signifying the place occupied by Christ at the Last Supper.[1] It can be so occupied only by one of greater sanctity than are those at the Second Table. It follows that for the purposes of this Romance the merit of Galahad was greater than that of the First Bishop of Christendom, who held the Warrant of his own Ordination from Christ Himself. When the fact was made public, Simeon and Moses speculated as to its truth and reason. Being sinners, they regarded it as false, and Moses undertook to occupy the seat if permission could be obtained from Joseph II. The latter was told by those who were parties to the conspiracy that a man counted among the sinners was worthy to take his seat at the Grail. Joseph was astonished, knowing under what circumstances he had crossed over to Britain; but his informants persisted, and though he could not believe in the goodness of Moses, he gave him leave to try. This was without reference to the Voice of the Grail, which was consulted on the occasion according to Robert de Borron, and it illustrates my previous statement that in the later Romance the Sacred Vessel rarely pronounces oracles or acts as a touchstone. Joseph, however, warned Moses himself, when the time came for the trial, not to make the attempt, unless he knew that he was worthy, as he would repent thereof, seeing that it was the Place of the Son of God. Moses was struck with terror but persisted, and, before he had sat long, seven burning hands came from Heaven, set him on fire like a dry bush, and carried him off through the air. Shame fell upon his sinful companions, who inquired whether he was lost or saved: they were told that they should see him again, and that then they would know his fate.[2]

At a later period, when the Company were approaching the forest of Darnantes, they were directed that they must enter therein, and were told that they should find Moses. In a valley they came presently upon a great house and, passing through open gates, they entered a spacious hall, wherein burned a great fire. Out of the fire came a voice, which begged Joseph to pray for the speaker, that his sufferings might be alleviated by the mercy of God. This was the voice of Moses. Joseph II, who was present, demanded whether he was saved or lost, and the answer was that still he had hope of grace. He had been transported by devils, who meant certainly to plunge him in hell; but a hermit compelled them to release him, as in spite of his sin he had not deserved endless torment. The fire was destined to encompass him till he was delivered by that Good Knight who would end the Adventures of the Grail. Alain, who was present also, asked more specifically who he was, and was told that it was his cousin Moses. Simeon also spoke to him, when he was advised, and Canaan—another of the evil

---

[1] It is obvious indeed that when the time of the Quest arrives Galahad, in taking the Siege Perilous, is given the place of Christ.
[2] Sommer, *Op. cit.*, I, pp. 247-249.

fellowship—that they should seek to be better than they were, and to be cleansed from sin by the Bishop. Joseph II and Alain prayed for Moses, that his suffering might be lessened. A beneficent rain came down into the fire, softening its fervour by extinguishing half thereof, so that the poor sufferer was eased greatly.[1] Simeon inquired how long such flames might endure, and was told by Moses that it would not be so long as he deserved, because he would be released by Galahad, who not alone would end the Adventures of the Grail but all those of Britain

In spite of the counsel which came to them from a source that illustrated so bitterly the neglect of warnings, Simeon and a certain Canaan not only remained without grace but made haste to complete that which remained for them to do in the order of heinous offence. Joseph of Arimathæa and some part of the Christian cohort had entered Scotland, where we have seen long ago that they were sustained by the Holy Grail. In this benefit of refection Simeon and Canaan were precluded by their condition from sharing, with the result that they had nothing to eat for two days and nights.[2] Simeon claimed that he had done more for God than either Joseph or Petrus, and that he was suffering for their sins: on the other hand, Canaan declared that he was punished for the deficiencies of his own immediate kindred. Simeon covenanted to take vengeance on Petrus and Canaan on his brethren. The issue was that, grievously and almost incurably, the Petrus of Borron's story was wounded in the neck with a poisoned knife, and the twelve brothers of Canaan were despatched with a sword. The visitation of these crimes is varied strangely in respect of severity, and it illustrates, I think, some vague and undeclared sanctity in the mission of Petrus. If so, it is a reflection from Robert de Borron, though in the later story there is no Brief from Heaven, or other Warrant, as the evident Seal of Mission. In any case, he who only wounded Petrus was transported, like Moses, by spirits of fire, while he who was a twelve-fold fratricide, by the comparative mercy of earthly judgment, was buried indeed alive, but with time to repent before death overtook him almost in the ordinary course.[3] Long and long afterwards, when Galahad le Fort, who had become King of Wales, was riding through that country, he saw a great fire burning in a dry ditch. A voice came therefrom and it proved to be that of Simeon, who was expiating in this manner his outrage on Petrus. At the same time—and again like Moses—he was not beyond redemption, and he entreated his auditor to found a place of religion, wherein monks could pray for his soul. Galahad le Fort promised to erect an abbey and to be buried himself therein. Simeon said further that his torment would cease when a Pure and Worthy Knight should come and extinguish the flames. This again would be he by whom the Adventures of the Holy Grail should be brought at last to their term.[4]

[1] *Op. cit.*, pp. 260–262.
[2] *Ib.*, p. 263.
[3] *Op. cit.*, pp. 262–267.
[4] *Ib.*, p. 283.

It is towards the close of the story that Petrus is mentioned first in the GRAND SAINT GRAAL, and is described merely as *Pieres uns parens Josephe*.[1] He is licensed on one occasion to carry the Holy Grail.[1] After the assault of Simeon, the wound of Petrus was examined and a healing by herbs was attempted; but this did more harm than good. He was left at length in the charge of a single Priest, while the Company proceeded on their way; but, seeing that he expected to die, he asked to be carried to the seashore and to be placed in a ship which was found lying thereby with its sails set. The Priest was not allowed to go further, and the vessel put out presently with its solitary occupant. He was taken to the Isle of Orkney, where ruled the Pagan King Orcaut, whose Daughter witnessed his arrival. She went on board the ship and so contrived that Petrus was healed in the end by a Christian prisoner who was in the hands of her father. As the issue of the whole adventure, the heathen King was converted; Petrus married the Daughter; he lived a long and worthy life as the successor of Orcaut; and he had a valiant Knight for his heir. He died in fullness of years and was buried at Orkney, in a Church dedicated to St. Philip.

It will be seen that if the author of the GRAND SAINT GRAAL designed in this account to supply the missing branch of Robert de Borron concerning Petrus, he again—and quite manifestly—told the wrong story, for setting aside all question of the written Warrant, the true destination of Petrus was not Orkney but Avalon, and there is no correspondence otherwise with the intimations of the Metrical Romance.

In nearly all those incidents which, from other points of view, are similar to some of Robert de Borron, the part assigned by the poem to Joseph of Arimathæa is transferred to the Son in this prose Romance which is its wresting rather than its extension. A notable instance is the demand for advice by Brons concerning his twelve boys. It is late in the story and long after the arrival of the Pilgrims in Britain that the question arises which appears pregnant with consequence in the Metrical Romance. Brons has been himself so insignificant throughout that his name appears scarcely, though he is entitled to sit with Joseph II, each on one side of the Vacant Seat at the Second Table. As in the earlier text, eleven of the sons expressed a desire to marry while the twelfth—being Alain le Gros—elected to lead a life of virginity.[2] Joseph II manifested great joy at the choice thus made and foreshadowed the reward which was to follow. It is indicated further by the fact that the Son, and not Brons, was directed to fish in the lake and obtain that slender catch which gave him thenceforward the title of the Rich Fisher. In this case, however, it was used by a miracle to feed those whose desert did not allow them to share in the graces and favours of the Holy Table.[3] When Joseph II was dying there stood Alain by his bedside, and, being asked why he was weeping, he answered that it was because he was to be left like a sheep that has lost its shepherd. He was told, however, that he himself should be the

---

[1] Sommer, I, p. 250.   [2] *Op. cit.*, p. 249.   [3] *Op. cit.*, pp. 251, 252.

THE VULGATE CYCLE OF THE HOLY GRAIL 193

shepherd after Joseph, having the Lordship of the Sacred Vessel, with power to deliver subsequently to another inheritor full of grace and goodness, on condition only that the Hallow remained in the land.[1]

We come in this manner to speak of the successions and genealogies, and in the first place concerning the Keepers of the Grail. Alain, by a curious disposition, died on the same day as Alphasan, the builder of Corbenic, and both were buried in a Church of that city dedicated to our Lady. The text at this point is a little vague in expression and has been interpreted wrongly; but the succeeding Warden was evidently Joshua—that brother of Alain who was most loved by him. He was followed in due course by his son Eminadap, who married the daughter of a King of Great Britain and had Carceloys as issue. The latter begot Manuiel, and from him sprang Lambor, whose death and that which followed I have mentioned previously. This was the first Maimed King of the Grail, and on him followed immediately one who was the Maimed King *par excellence* of suffering and miracle of final healing—that is to say, Pellehan. But the GRAND SAINT GRAAL says that his wounding was in the battle of Rome, and it knows nothing therefore of the Dolorous Stroke inflicted by Balyn. Seeing, however, that both texts testify that Galahad will heal, and he only, I think it must be inferred that the two accounts refer to the same person, who must be distinguished from King Pelles, though there is an inclination in some criticism to conclude otherwise, and I have shared it tentatively. The genealogy is quite clear that King Pelles was son of Pellehan, and there is not any real difficulty about the son succeeding in the life of the father, as this occurs in the case of Joseph II and is the rule rather than the exception in the counter-succession of the Perceval Quests. It follows from the GRAND SAINT GRAAL that four of the Kings whom I have enumerated were called Rich Fishers in succession and that all of them reigned in *Terre Forayne*, which the VULGATE MERLIN terms—or for which it substitutes—Lystenoys.

The other genealogies are useful only in so far as they shew the descent of the persons-in-chief who appear in the Vulgate Chronicles. The most important is that of Nasciens, which leads up through many names—but they are names only—to King Ban of Benoic, the father of Lancelot, and hence to Lancelot himself, as well as Galahad. The *Haut Prince* was descended therefore on the male side from the royal line of Sarras, over which he reigned himself after the Quest was finished; on the female side he was descended from Joseph of Arimathæa, through Galahad le Fort, as the ROMANCE OF LANCELOT shews. Sir Gawain also is represented as coming from this root, which was that of King David; but his descent was through Petrus, the genealogy of whom is clouded rather deeply in the text;[2] as it is indeed in the Romance of Borron.

At the conclusion of the GRAND SAINT GRAAL the story professes to turn to the life of Merlin. Two of its codices contain a long interspersed

[1] *Ib.*, p. 286. [2] *Op. cit.*, p. 281.

digression concerning the two countries belonging to Mordrains and Nasciens after they had departed therefrom. Their power and influence were much increased under Grimaud, the son of Mordrains. When Sarras was destroyed, with the exception of the Spiritual Palace, it was rebuilt more splendidly than ever. These things do not concern us, for in dealing with the great prolix Romance I think that my summary has been confined, in accordance with my design, to those matters which belong to the Mystery of the Grail as it is manifested in the Vulgate Cycle, and, where it has been possible, to the Eucharistic side of that Mystery as the most holy motive of all my long research. On this subject there is one thing further to say. The doctrine of Transubstantiation, as it is presented in the GRAND SAINT GRAAL, and its continual transition into the notion of physical sustenance, are things which scandalise rather than discounsel the soul; but as we saw in the poem of Borron that Eucharist and Reliquary were alike understood spiritually, so here it will be found in the last sifting that the spiritual side emerges also and becomes at times prominent. When Joseph II, in obedience to the Heavenly Voice, departed from Sarras and its King, that he might preach the new faith to the Gentiles, it came about in the course of the journey that provisions were wanting. In this extremity he knelt before the Ark, wherein was the Holy Vessel, and implored the help of God. Following the directions which he received, cloths were laid on the greensward, and the people took their places. The elder Joseph, pursuing his care of the physical bodies, ordained that his Son should take the Grail in his hands and follow him round the cloths while he circumambulated three times, when—this being accomplished—all who were pure of heart would be filled with the rare sweetness of the world. This Office took place at the Hour of Prime; the Father and Son sat down, with a vacant place between them —as if something were lacking which at a fitting time subsequently would make perfect all holy ministry; the Vessel was covered with Paten and Corporal;[1] and the result was that those who were privileged to take part were filled with Divine Grace, " so that they could neither conceive nor desire anything beyond it." That was a refection in which material nourishment shared not at all, and though the episode does not occur in all the codices, there is something that corresponds to its equivalent. An instance in point is found in Mordrains, the King, who, after he has attained all earthly knowledge, and has received as the price of attainment the orbicular wound of Plato, is nourished through the centuries by the Eucharist, as Anfortas in the German Cycle and the *alter ego* of both in the CONTE DEL GRAAL. There are otherwise indications, and they obtain throughout the Vulgate Chronicles, that the proximity of the Holy Grail transformed the earthly festival into an experience *in extasis* and that the good things here below became a*r bona Domini in terra viventium*.

---

[1] The Holy Grail was therefore a Chalice, or at least was used as such.

IV

THE VULGATE MERLIN

A CONSPICUOUS break notwithstanding between the EARLY HISTORY OF MERLIN, which ends by saying that King Arthur held his land and kingdom long in peace, and the VULGATE MERLIN, which begins by reciting how the nobles who had acknowledged him unwillingly went against him into prolonged rebellion, does not hinder the Vulgate codification from prefixing the EARLY HISTORY to its later text. But the main derivations, as it stands, are from the GRAND SAINT GRAAL and the appurtenances thereof, including the prose LANCELOT. We are concerned only with the text in respect of its Grail references, and of the content otherwise it will be sufficient therefore to say that there is embodied an exhaustive account of King Arthur's Wars with the Saxons, a certain group of adventures of the less indubitably romantic kind,[1] and thereafter the various circumstances which lead up to the internment of Merlin, through the wiles and enchantments of Vivien. In this manner it is the close of the Prophet's chronicle, though it is still only the early history of Arthur.

Here, as elsewhere, the re-editing of Romances in the Grail interest is to be distinguished from innumerable alterations made otherwise by various transcribers but to which no ulterior motive need be attributed. Perhaps the most signal instance of all the major editing is the production of two sequels executed independently, to the MERLIN of Robert de Borron, both of which were made less or more exclusively in the interests which I have mentioned, while both also are ascribed falsely to the same hand. We might elucidate better the VULGATE and HUTH MERLIN could one of them be accepted as carrying further forward the Borron Tradition and thus leading up to a Perceval Quest, whether that of the Didot-Modena manuscripts or another—as, for example, the PERLESVAUS, itself presupposing an early history of the Welsh hero. But the derivatives of both texts offer insuperable difficulties in respect of this course. At the same time the process of codification is nowhere complete in the literature. We must assume, for example, on the basis of textual criticism, that the prose LANCELOT had in some form enriched already the Cycle when the VULGATE MERLIN came into existence; but in several particulars the Merlin allusions in the LANCELOT do not correspond with anything in those later Merlin stories with which we are concerned here. These, on the other hand,

[1] As for example (1) the circumstances under which Arthur begot Mordred on the body of his half-sister, wife of King Lot of Orkney; (2) those of his own marriage to Guinevere, daughter of Leodegan, King of Cameliard; complicated (3) by the fact that the latter had a natural daughter of the same name whom a plot attempts to substitute for the Bride chosen by the King. It may be added that in the HUTH MERLIN Mordred is the lawful son of Lot and a daughter of the Duke of Tintagel. See the French text. p. 120, but it is contradicted by *ib.*, p. 147.

when they reflect elements that are particular to the LANCELOT, may be reproducing in mere summary or they may offer new materials by way of variation over details.

The VULGATE MERLIN says that God has given to the Prophet that skill and discretion which he possesses so to assist him that he shall accomplish in fine the Adventures of the Holy Grail, which Adventures are predestined to take place in the time of King Arthur, while Blaise, the Hermit and Scribe, shall live to behold the end. This is true in respect of the DIDOT-MODENA PERCEVAL but not of the other Quests, in which this personage is forgotten, or is lost at least among many recording clerks. But as it follows from the reference, by intimation, that Merlin will not himself survive, the Vulgate text cannot be said to lead up to that document. In the interminable account of the Wars with Rion, a Saxon King, there is some stress laid on the achievements of Nasciens, who is the second of that name and not only had been famous in the reign of Uther Pendragon but still surpassed all others in Chivalry. His admission into the Fellowship of the Round Table took place in Arthurian days. He was, moreover, (1) a cousin of Perceval le Gallois, (2) of near kinship to Joseph of Arimathæa, (3) a cousin of Celidoine, and (4) a relation of Pelles, King of Lystenois. Here the derivation is of course from the GRAND SAINT GRAAL; but the genealogy is a little distracted. Subsequently Nasciens is said to have had Galahad in his keeping, which statement is reflected into the Welsh Quest.[1] Later still, he had the story in his charge, and by ordinance of the Great Master he announced that which he found therein—otherwise, in the Record of Blaise.

There is more than one reference to Elaine, the Daughter of King Pelles of Castle Corbenic, the niece of King Fisher and of Alain, who was wounded through both thighs by an avenging spear. She was the fairest lady in the land and had the Blessed Vessel in her keeping till the time of Galahad's conception.[2] After what manner she was dispossessed of her High Office the text covenants to declare at a later time; but seeing that it fails herein, it shall be reserved on my own part for the Branch which belongs to Galahad. We hear also concerning a son of King Pelles who—as in the ROMANCE OF LANCELOT—is named Eleazar. At the age of fifteen years he told his father that he should never be made a Knight till the best Knight of the World should give him his arms and the accolade after three years of service. In return for the dignity of Chivalry he believes that he shall take the Knight to the country of King Pelles and the House of the Grail. At this time the King's Daughter, though Bearer of the Sacred Vessel, is only seven years old.[3] Seeing that Galahad during his brief career

---

[1] The reference may be to what must be called the hidden life of Galahad before he came to Court: in any case Nasciens does not figure in the Great Quest.

[2] It is said also that she was the wisest woman of *la Bloie Bretaigne*, surpassing even Guinevere, the wife of Arthur.—See LESTOIRE DE MERLIN in Sommer's VULGATE VERSION OF THE ARTHURIAN ROMANCES, II, p. 159.

[3] *Ib.*, p. 346.

THE VULGATE CYCLE OF THE HOLY GRAIL 197

of Knighthood does not confer the High Order on any Squire in his service, save only Melyas de Lyle, Son of the King of Denmark, and much less on one who would be his uncle according to the flesh, whom also he was destined to meet in the Grail Castle at the term of all, we have here a variant of the Legend which differs in certain respects from any extant chronicle of the Perfect Knight. It is otherwise obvious that the *Haut Prince* is not the Best Knight in question; nor is it in fact Perceval, on whom the title is conferred in his own stories. It comes about indeed that in the end Eleazar serves Gawain and receives the accolade from him, though he was never Best Knight of the World, nor did Eleazar ever conduct him to the Grail Castle.[1]

I do not know what construction is to be placed upon the position of King Pelles: to all intents and purposes he is the Warden-in-Chief of the Grail in the QUEST OF GALAHAD; but neither there nor in the VULGATE MERLIN is he called the Rich Fisher, which is the characteristic title of the Warden. The Romance with which we are here and now concerned tells us, this notwithstanding, that he is spoken of as the Rich King, which seems by way of alternative: he is also a full noble Ruler and a true one. But there is under his charge King Pellenore of the Welsh Lands, that is to say, Pellehan, who is sick and will never be healed till there is manifested one who shall bring to an end the Adventures of the Holy Grail. This comes to pass at the close of the times of Galahad. But there is another brother, who is Alain of the *Terre Forayne*: he is in sickness also, and will never be cured till the best knight of all Britain shall ask him why he is stricken by that malady and what it is that will help him. It follows that there is here an analogue of Perceval's Question; but it is never asked in the sequel, nor do we hear further of Alain.

In the VULGATE MERLIN the place of the Grail is Corbenic; it is situated in the realm of Lystenois, which might signify Lyonesse; and just as we know that the Castle is one of perilous and even fatal adventure, so the kingdom to which it belongs is in nowise a region of peace; and I have said already that its Ruler is a King in Warfare. The Romance contains few other references to the Sacred Vessel and the History or the Quest thereof. The tidings of the Grail in Britain are still tidings only; the Quest is still not a search after the place of the Hallows, but of Knights who are proper to undertake it.[2] On matters of so-called early history we hear that Joseph of Arimathæa received the Blood from the side of Christ into the Sacred Vessel when the body was still hanging on the Cross—representing a Tradition that differs from the Lesser Chronicles, though it is reflected from one of the visions in the GRAND SAINT GRAAL. We hear further that the Grail came from Heaven above into the city of Sarras, which may be a description by inadvertence, or it may represent a reflection from some

---
[1] *Op. cit.*, p. 389.
[2] It is evident that the rumour grows from more to more; and seeing that Vessel and Lance can be found only by the best and bravest Knight, all those who are of fair report are drawn to the Court of King Arthur.—*Cp. cit.*, p. 335.

source which corresponds to the antecedents of Wolfram—if any, outside Chrétien. The Spear which opened the side of Christ was brought to Logres, presumably—for it is not stated—by him who was the first to Consecrate and offer the Eucharistic Sacrifice: that is to say, by the Second Joseph.

So far in fine as the VULGATE MERLIN can be said to end at all[1]—seeing that it stops or breaks off without redeeming its pledges—the close is taken soon after the enchantment of Merlin by arts of his own instruction given to the Lady of the Lake.[2] The Record of Blaise ceases for want of materials; but in the meantime the clerks of the Court of King Arthur have taken up the story in a sense, though their task is confined to registrations of prowess exhibited by those who are admitted newly to the Round Table, and are therefore at once Protagonists of earthly Chivalry spiritualised and possible seekers for the Grail.

V

THE GREAT PROSE LANCELOT

BY many ways do all the antecedent texts of the Vulgate Chronicles lead up, in the hands of their editors, to the Romance of Lancelot. Therefrom, or therein, all reflect, according to their respective measures, and itself is the great text which goes before the Romance of Galahad, as a Royal Prince may herald the King of All. The pseudo-base of the story in respect of early Grail History is the GRAND SAINT GRAAL; but some of its references have no authority in that document. In comparison with its vast extent, the allusions to the Sacred Vessel are rare and brief. I will take all the necessary points in their order,[3] beginning with two pregnant statements, the first of which is conclusive as to the historical source; for it is said that the Holy Grail was that Dish in which Christ ate the Paschal Lamb with His disciples. But the story is late chronologically in the sequence; it reflected much; its ambition was to include all Arthurian Chivalry in its province; and none knew better than the successive authors, who are thought to have welded it into one whole, that the true Service of the Sacred Vessel took place at no festival of earthly meats, but at an Arch-Natural Mass. It is haunted therefore with the same idea as we shall find in the LONGER PROSE PERCEVAL—that what besides it was, the Grail was also a Chalice, and it is so described accordingly in one of the later branches. In evidence

---

[1] The last recorded event is the birth of Lancelot. *Ib.*, p. 465.
[2] That is to say, Vivien. But it may be noted that Morgan le Fay, who is one of Arthur's sisters, learns many of Merlin's crafts. *Ib.*, p. 254.
[3] There are many others and many casual references which trench on familiar ground. It is said, for example, that the Adventures of the Siege Perilous and the Holy Grail will put an end to those of Logres. Sommer's Vulgate LANCELOT, II, p. 26.

of this it may be noted that it is apparently the Dove's Censer in the Story of Lancelot which brings the good meat and drink. The second statement occurs in a printed codex, and scholarship, which misses so little within its own province, has contrived to overlook this: the book says, however, that the Natural Grail is to be distinguished from that which is Supernatural; and this I take to mean that on the one side there is the Festival of the Feeding Dish and on the other the Feast Mystical of Transubstantiation, at the revelation of the whole mystery in the QUEST OF GALAHAD, foreshadowed, as a thing done out of due season, at the Ordination of Joseph II in the old time of Sarras. Beyond both, there is the last experience of the *Haut Prince* in the so-called Spiritual City.

It will not be found, otherwise than as I have here specified, that the Grail elements differ so much from the earlier versions as the actuating sentiments regarding the heroes of the Quest and the qualifications thereto belonging. A certain new spirit has entered—perhaps even a higher quality of the Secret Life of the Church—and it has moderated, among other things, the final aim regarding the Stewards of the Grail and the persons with and for whom it is represented as sojourning on earth. Speaking of the Romance as a whole, it may be said that it is a Wonder-Book rather than a Book of Initiation, though at certain points it embodies very high Mysteries. According to its own description, it is a branch of the Great Book of the Holy Grail; but the implied reason is that Lancelot was the Father of Galahad. Make as it may for confusion, it is just to add here that, in this connection, one of the unprinted manuscripts speaks of Perceval as the leader and term of all stories told about other Knights: it was he who achieved the Great Quest; but his story also is a branch of the High Story concerning the Grail, which is the head and crown of all stories. This would seem to indicate that Galahad was not the final hero of the Quest, so far as this codex is concerned, but it may mean also and more probably that he had his own great place at the last consummation, or that he was an intermediate seeker, as were Lancelot also and Gawain.

We shall find in the HUTH MERLIN, firstly that it has allusions to various occurrences in the QUEST OF GALAHAD which are missing in the extant Romance, and, secondly, that much of its material is derived from the GREAT PROSE LANCELOT. So also in this text there are references to a succeeding branch of the Quest which we have now no means of checking; but they are not identical throughout with those in the HUTH MERLIN. It is said (1) that the story will recur in this part to the Knight Meliadus, but we hear nothing concerning him; (2) that it will speak of Helain the White, who became Emperor of Constantinople, but this it does not do; (3) that many marvels concerning the Tower of Merlin will be recounted therein, but we hear nothing; (4) that Orpheus, a certain enchanter, is doomed to remain in the Castle of the Holy Grail, with two snakes about his neck, until the Quest has been achieved; but he is forgotten entirely therein. These items may be contrasted with those which have been specified in respect of the VULGATE MERLIN: if there are others, as a more exhaustive analysis would find, and this assuredly, I believe that my purpose has been served within the measure of reason; and I will turn therefore to some, further Grail references found in the LANCELOT, and of which we hear otherwise.

There are several intimations concerning the close of the Adventurous Times in Great Britain,[1] and the occupation of the Siege Perilous at the Round Table: the commencement of these times was on the occasion of the war declared by Uther Pendragon against King Urien. There is also a certain Knight, named Elias, who carried two swords, after the manner of Balyn: one of them was enclosed in a priceless scabbard, and is said to be that in the old days which pierced the loins of Joseph of Arimathæa and was broken therein, as narrated in the GRAND SAINT GRAAL. It was destined not to be resoldered except by the Lord of Chivalry, who was to put an end to the Adventurous Times, with all the Wonders and Mysteries of the Holy Vessel.[2]

A few other points will be taken best with the personal history of Lancelot, though it is not within my province to provide a formal analysis of the Romance itself. Lancelot was the son of King Ban of Benoic, and his mother Helen was of the race of Joseph of Arimathæa, through whom she was of the line of King David. It is said therefore that, through his Mother, Lancelot had the same blood in his veins as the King of Heaven Himself had deigned to take.[3]

His baptismal name was Galahad, and, according to the HUTH MERLIN, Lancelot was that which he received in Confirmation, though I find no record concerning this Sacrament in his own Romance. He was carried away in his infancy by one of the Ladies of the Lake:[4] she is really that Vivien who deceived Merlin, and who, under a cloud of poetic modernism, is familiar to the readers of Tennyson. The part which she plays through all the Tale of Chivalry is out of true kinship with what we have been disposed to conceive as she is pictured in the departed laureate's glass of vision. By the knowledge which she derived from Merlin she entered that unincorporated Hierarchy of Fairyland of which we hear in the Books of Chivalry: she became a fay-lady, which signifies not an extra-human being of some minor or elemental order, but a woman proficient in Magic. It should be noted here that whereas, in the ordinary acceptation, a fairy may correspond either to male or female, the term is never used in the Arthurian Books except with reference to a woman. For example, the Fountain of Fairies, which is mentioned once in the LANCELOT, received that name because beautiful unknown ladies had been seen thereat.[5] The Lake

---

[1] Sommer, *Op. cit.*, III, p. 88; IV, p. 27.
[2] *Ib.*, IV, p. 324 *et seq.*
[3] *Op. cit.*, III, 12–17.
[4] *Ib.*, 22. The lake was no lake but an illusion of enchantment which concealed and shielded also the Lady of the Lake's abode.
[5] Compare the Prologue to the CONTE DEL GRAAL, Potvin, *Op. cit.*, Vol. II, at the beginning.

THE VULGATE CYCLE OF THE HOLY GRAIL 201

into which the child was carried was therefore a Lake of Magic, concealing from public view the Palace or Manor in which his guardian dwelt, and the great park-land about it. The account of the region within this water of enchantment recalls one of the romantic episodes in LE ROMAN DE JAUFRE; and, speaking generally, there are distinct analogies between this comparatively unknown Provençal poem and other Tales of the Round Table.[1]

Lancelot remained in the charge of the Lady of the Lake until he was eighteen. About this period she told him the story of his ancestor Joseph, and also of Joseph's son, the first Galahad, who became a King of that country which afterwards was called Wales.[2] She referred to King Pelles of Lystenoys and his brother, a second and later Alain le Gros, who had never ceased to maintain themselves in high honour and glory before the world and in the sight of God. As regards his own future course, she forewarned him that he was called to carry to their term many wonderful adventures, while those which he did not achieve would remain over for a Knight who was yet unborn, that is to say, for the last and true Galahad. But of the Grail she did not tell him, though at a later time he heard of the tomb of Lucan, connected with a House of Religion, wherein was buried the godson of Joseph of Arimathæa, who was once charged with the guardianship of the Sacred Vessel. The HUTH MERLIN says, however, that it was a granddaughter of the First Keeper, which seems to accord better with the General Tradition.

Before parting with Lancelot, the Lady of the Lake gave him a wand or ring[3]—for the codices differ—which had the power of dissolving enchantments, presumably other than her own; and it served him in good stead at many junctures. Thus equipped, she led him forth into the world, accompanied by an amazing retinue,[4] and repaired to the Court of King Arthur, where he was Knighted,[5] and where, in due time, he was entered as a Companion of the Round Table, a reception which was characterised by considerable ceremonial grandeur. So passed he into the World of Chivalry; but through the glory of his after-life, and through the scandal of his unhappy, over-measured, too faithful love, we have no call to follow him. Before we come—in another section—to the great event of his history, outside these particular vocations, there are only three further points to be noted. On one occasion he has a vision of his ancestors, namely, Nasciens, Celidoine, the second Nasciens, Alain le Gros and Jonas, who begot the first Lancelot, who was himself father to King Ban of Benoic. But it will be observed that this is on the male side, and is therefore without prejudice to his derivation on the mother's side from the *radix Jesse*. On another occasion Lancelot visited the tomb of the first Galahad, King of Wales.[6]

---

[1] See Marie Lafon's prose translation entitled: LES AVENTURES DU CHEVALIER JAUFRE ET DE LA BELLE BRUNISSENDE, pp. 122-135. 1856.
[2] Sommer, *Op. cit.*, III, pp. 117, 118.
[3] *Op. cit.*, III, p. 123.
[4] Appendix I, Note 14.
[5] Sommer, *Op. cit.*, III, p. 127.
[6] *Op. cit.*, IV, p. 175.

He saw also the burning sepulchre of Simeon, and spoke with that victim of the centuries, who told him that the Knight who should deliver him would be of his own kindred, and as nearly as possible the very flesh of Lancelot.[1] It is said in explanation that Simeon was the father of Moses and the nephew of Joseph, all which is in opposition to Robert de Borron, though it reproduces literally the GRAND SAINT GRAAL. Moses was tormented in a similar tomb; but owing to the prayers of Joseph both had experienced a certain mitigation, and their delivery in thirty years was insured at last.[2] Lancelot removed the body of the first Galahad, which was transported to Wales and reinterred with great honour. The third point concerns the visit of Gawain and Hector to a certain graveyard which they are counselled not to enter unless one of them is the recreant knight whose evil living has caused him to forfeit the honour of achieving the Adventures of the Grail.[3] The reference is to Lancelot, and in the graveyard is a marble tomb which contains not only Simeon but his accomplice Canaan and the twelve brothers whom they immolated. While this appears to stultify the previous account of Simeon's place of purgation it is conclusive as to the disqualification of Lancelot for the Great Quest. Had he never loved the Queen, he would not have begotten Galahad, for whom no office would have remained, seeing that he himself was the Exotic Flower of Chivalry, Palm of Faith and Cedar of Purity. But, as things were, the great light of Lancelot was clouded deeply, nor ever shone freely until that term of all when he was received into a Priestly Sanctuary of the Official Church and was clothed at last in incense. It is certain that, speaking generally of the Vulgate Chronicles, there was no true light of Gawain, though some of the Romances issued from the ministry of Nature have pictured him in glowing colours. Subject to one great and cryptic exception, the day of Chrétien and Wauchier had given way to the day of the prose LANCELOT, and Gawain had been stripped of nearly all his graces, a process first begun in the ROMANCE OF TRISTRAM. Perhaps it may be said that albeit he saw something according to the CONTE DEL GRAAL, therein is an episode of personation, on which I have dwelt shortly, though it was not consciously to the hero himself. In Heinrich's poem he enters only into a world of ghosts. In the prose LANCELOT he is characterised by a constitutional incapacity, to which the Galahad Quest adds impenitence in evil-doing. The picture of Sir Bors—on the other hand—is one of great beauty; but it does not carry with it any particular significance, except that of a witness on his way back into the world. Among the Grail heroes we are reduced therefore, as we have seen and shall see otherwise further, to Perceval and Galahad. Of these two there is little doubt that Perceval was the first in time, or that in a certain sense Galahad was an afterthought. I use the expression so that I may introduce the more acceptable view that this Elect Knight represents a later but exceedingly express intention, as if it were the

---

[1] Sommer, *Op. cit.*, IV, p. 176.   [2] *Ib.*, p. 177.   [3] *Ib.*, pp. 339–341.

design of the Legend to say that a day would come when that Arthurian Sacrament of which I have spoken previously, would be communicated at last not only to the world without, but that the Official Church would receive also, on its knees, acknowledging that there are Great Consecrations. If, without seeming too fantastic, I may refer to an old symbol which has no special connection with the present order of ideas, Galahad is like the horn of the quintessence in the microcosmic and alchemical star, while the four other horns are the four aspects of the Symbolical Legend of Perceval, being (1) the DIDOT-MODENA PERCEVAL; (2) the CONTE DEL GRAAL; (3) the LONGER PROSE PERCEVAL; and (4) the PARZIVAL of Wolfram. It does no real outrage to the order of time if I say that these aspects represent, figuratively speaking, the growth of the Tradition. The DIDOT-MODENA PERCEVAL may be doubtless later than Chrétien, and from him may have borrowed something; but the two texts are near enough in time to make the question of priority, at least to an extent, unimportant. Let me endeavour to compare for a moment the intention of this strange pentagram in literature. Collectively or individually its documents are best taken in connection with one another, and in conjunction also with those which lead up to them. It is only the LONGER PROSE PERCEVAL which stands to some extent alone in the Northern French Cycle, though it has certain connections with the GRAND SAINT GRAAL. In the German Cycle the PARZIVAL is by no means without antecedents, for apart from the alleged hand of Kyot de Provence we can trace at least the analogies with Chrétien, though Wolfram scouted his version. Finally, we have the Galahad Legend, as if the closing were taken in a superlative Grade of Romance.

As in the CONTE DEL GRAAL, so in the Romance of Lancelot, there is one visit paid by Gawain to the Grail Castle, and it begins abruptly with an adventure at a pavilion by a certain fountain.[1] Gawain, who is actor-in-chief, reached a Castle subsequently in some annex or quarter of which he found a maiden in the durance of a scalding bath, wherefrom no one could save her except the highest typical example of Earthly Knighthood.[2] Gawain was not Lancelot—for whom the adventure was reserved—and he failed therefore, for which he was promised shame to ensue quickly. He was received with pomp in the Castle, and came into the presence of the King, by whom he was welcomed after the true manner of Chivalry. In a word, he was at Corbenic, the Grail Castle, and the herald of the secret ministry entered in the shape of a Dove, bearing a censer in its beak. This vision was momentary only, and was not repeated; but it served as a sign for the Company to take their seats at the tables, and this was followed by the entrance of a Maiden —their daughter, fairest among women—who carried the Chalice of the Grail, in her passage through the hall replenishing the dishes and filling the place with sweet odours. After what manner this multiplication of loaves and fishes takes place does not appear—a feature which

[1] *Op. cit.*, IV, p. 341.   [2] *Ib.*, p. 342.

characterises nearly all the coincident Legends of this particular type. It is worth a passing note that the LANCELOT is the only text in which the Grail Bearer is unaccompanied entirely. So much was Gawain bespelled by the Maiden's beauty that he had no eyes for anything else. She departed at length; and he, coming to himself, found that, for some fault which he could not identify, he only was left without refection of any kind—even as the evil doers in the Company of Joseph. The meal proceeded in complete silence, and was disconsolate enough for the hero, who began to feel already the working of that shame which was promised him. At the end of the supper the whole Company departed, still without any word, and a dwarf—who tried to chastise him, because of his presence in that part of the building—bade him at length go in search of some other chamber, where no one would see him. He remained, however, in the hall, and there had a certain partial vision of a Grail Service. The presence of the Sacred Vessel healed him not only of a grievous wound which he had received from a spear a little earlier in the narrative, but also of various hurts in a long combat with an unknown Knight in the hall. I omit any special account of this meeting, except that there again Gawain was attacked because he refused to depart. I omit also a clumsy parable concerning a dragon who gave birth to a vast progeny and afterwards strove with a leopard, only to be destroyed in the end by her own children, who perished likewise in the struggle. In a state of exhaustion Gawain at length fell asleep, and found on waking in the morning that he was being drawn through the public streets of the city in a vile cart. After being pelted with filth, he was released ultimately, and arrived at the hold of one whom men termed the Secret Hermit. From him he ascertained that he had been at the Grail Castle, which appears to be new tidings. Of the Sacred Vessel and its Mysteries he learned nothing, though it was foretold that he should know soon; but this promise does not seem to be fulfilled.[1]

Of such is the message of the literature as it moves slowly and heavily towards the greater heights of its root-conception. It should be added that whereas in the prose LANCELOT Gawain is covered thus with disdain, the Romance of Galahad paints him in darker colours. I do not know why there was such a revulsion of feeling in respect of one who in certain texts appears as the Knight of Earthly Courtesy, and who assuredly in the CONTE DEL GRAAL is scarcely less entitled to consideration than Perceval himself.

After another manner is it dealt to another Knight, who visited the Castle also, but he was the Diadem of Chivalry which at that time had been exalted in the world of Logres.[2] By this I mean that he was Lancelot, and he arrived not only as an expected guest, but as one whose advent had been decreed and led up to from the first times of the Mystery. It was then that the great parable of the adventurous Times

---

[1] Sommer, *Op. cit.*, IV, pp. 343-348. Note also concerning the Praise of Gawain, p. 358. [2] *Ib.*, III, p. 105 *et seq.*

passed into that other parable concerning Times of Enchantment, because it was understood before everything, and was accepted also, that the faith of King Ban's Son was with the heart of the Queen for ever, and so utterly that, in the sub-surface mind of Romance, it had even moved somewhere as if towards a lower sacramental order; or—without being condoned therein—it was thought to have carried within it an element of redemption. Dedicated and vowed as he was, no other willing union was possible; and hence the offices of Enchantment were needed to bring about the conception of Galahad by the Daughter of the House of the Grail, with Lancelot as the morganatic Father, thus insuring the genealogical legitimacy of the last Recipient of the Mysteries.

Of this conception I propose to speak in another section, because the LANCELOT dissolves into the QUEST, of which the first condition is the birth of Galahad.

VI

A PREFACE OR INTRODUCTORY PORTION APPERTAINING TO ALL THE QUESTS

THERE is a certain sense in which we can say that the Knight of old was consecrated like the Priest of old, and the PONTIFICALE ROMANUM perpetuates to this day the official mode of his hallowing. There is an arming in its high observance and there is an authentic accolade. Declared or undeclared, the intention was that even warfare should be dedicated to the high ends of the Church, as if the implied covenant of battle were that a man should be so prepared through all his days that no sudden or violent death should find him unfitted for his transit. The causes of strife are many, and some of them are doubtful enough; but clothed thus in the armour of salvation the natural-born hero experienced a kind of rebirth and came forth, so far as he himself was concerned, a Soldier of the Cross. One section at least in the romantic literature of Chivalry was devoted to this ideal, and better than any formal Catechism of Doctrine and Conduct did it uphold the Greater Purpose of the Church and illustrate the hypotheses of its practice. That section was the Quest of the Holy Grail in its proper understanding, and on the authority of this fact I can say that the branch itself became a search after high sanctity expressed in the form of Romance: as such it does not differ from the Quest-in-chief of holiness.

These statements—which are introduced like an interlude or a section apart and as if extra-judicial—would sound strangely in the ears of those who have preceded me, and it must be understood that, of course, I am speaking of things as they are found at their highest in the great texts; but the evidence is there: it is there also in terms that it is impossible to elude and impossible also to discount. In respect of the CONTE DEL GRAAL, we must surrender to Nature the things which are Nature's; but the LONGER PROSE PERCEVAL says that of God moveth its High History;[1] and I say likewise—but in a more exalted degree still—concerning the QUEST OF GALAHAD. Were it otherwise, the literature of the Grail would be like the records of any other princes of this world, and my predilections would have nothing therein.

It was only by slow stages that the course of the literature rose up to that height at which it found rather than created the ideal of Galahad. We may take as our most obvious illustration of the developing process one crucial point which characterises the earlier Perceval Quests, and this is the loves of the hero. The earlier branches of the CONTE DEL GRAAL shew little conscience on the subject of restraint, the deportment of the hero being simply a question of opportunity. I know that we are dealing with a period when the natural passions were condoned rather easily, though the Church had intervened to consecrate the Rite of Marriage after an especial manner. Hence it was no great stigma for a hero of Chivalry to be born out of wedlock, or to beget sons of desire who would shine in his light and their own subsequently. The ideal of virginity remained, all this notwithstanding, so that the makers of Romance knew well enough where the instituted Counsels of Perfection lay. It is comparatively late in the Cycles that ascetic purity became an indefectible title to success in the Quest of the Holy Grail, about which time Gawain and Lancelot were relegated to their proper places—ridicule and confusion, in the one case, and final, though not irreverent, disqualification in the other.

The DIDOT-MODENA PERCEVAL offers a frigid quality of abstinence, apart from either sympathy or enlightenment, and without one touch of grace to make it kindred with the ardours and solitudes of the Divine Life. The poem of Gerbert preserves the hero's virginity even on his marriage night; but the precaution—considering the texts which he had elected to follow—has the aspect of a leap in the dark. Wolfram insures the chastity of Parzival by introducing the marriage of his Questing Knight at an early stage. The LONGER PROSE PERCEVAL is like Heaven, knowing neither marriage nor giving in marriage, or at least nuptials are so utterly made in Heaven that they are not reflected on earth. Blanchefleur has disappeared entirely; and it is never supposed that the Quest would be achieved in perfection by one who was not a virgin. If we turn now to the story of Galahad, we shall find that the Quest of the Holy Grail has become an unearthly experiment. There is illumination, there is sanctity, there is ecstasy; and the greatest of these is ecstasy, because it is the term of the others. All the high researches end in a rapture, and thereby is that change of location which does not mean passage through space. I believe that the author

---

[1] *Et de Dieu si vient* (*si muet*, according to the Berne MS.) *li haus contes del Graal.* Potvin, *Op. cit.*, I, p. 2.

of the Great Quest knew what he was doing when—leaving nothing outside—he so transmuted all, and assuredly in the order of Romance he spoke as no man had spoken before him.

Now, seeing that all subjects bring us back to the one subject ; that in spite, for example, of any scandalous histories, every Official Congregation calls us, from afar or near, to the Secret Church ; so, at whatever point we may begin, I affirm that every Quest takes us ultimately to that of Galahad. It would seem therefore that this is the crown of all. If Galahad had come in the good time instead of in the evil, the Grail would have been set up for adoration before the whole face of Logres. But the Quest says that the world was not worthy, though the PARZIVAL seems to say : " Behold, I am with you always."

Of Perceval and his great experiment there are several phases : of Galahad there is one only, led up to by many Romances, but represented in fine by a single transcendent text. This is the quintessence and transmutation of everything, allocating all seekers—Perceval, Bors, Lancelot, Gawain—to their proper spheres, over whom shines Galahad as an Exalted Horn in the Great Pentagram of Chivalry. Of the Perceval Quest there are two major versions ; one of them, as I have noted already, is like an alternative conclusion to the Cycle of the Vulgate Chronicles ; and one—which is the German PARZIVAL—all antecedents notwithstanding, is something set apart by itself in a peculiar House of Mystery. It is the story of the natural man taken gradually to the ethical heights. There is also a third quest, that of the DIDOT-MODENA PERCEVAL, which, amidst many insufficiencies, is important for several reasons after its own manner—that is to say, because of its hypothetical genealogy. The fourth is the CONTE DEL GRAAL, and this—apart from Gerbert—is of no importance symbolically, though it is a great and powerful talisman of archaic poetry. The truth is that for all the high things there are many substitutes, after the manner of colourable pretences, and many transcripts, as out of the Language of the Angels into that of man, after the same way that the great external Churches have expressed the Mysteries of Doctrine in words of one syllable for children who are learning to read. But the absolute and direct message of the things most high, coming in the name of these, is commonly alone. In fine, it sometimes happens that as from any corner of the veil the prepared eyes can look through and perceive something of the immeasurable region which lies beyond the normal faculties of sense, so there are Mysteries of Books which are in no way sufficient in themselves, but they contain elements and portents of all those great things about which it is given the heart to conceive. Among these are the Grail Books in the forms which present the Legend at its highest.

VII

THE QUEST OF THE HIGH PRINCE

LET us now set before our minds the image of the Grail Castle, having a local habitation and a name on the mountain-side of Corbenic, somewhere in South-West Wales.[1] The dweller-in-chief of this Sanctuary is the Keeper of the Hallows, holding by lineal descent from the first times of the Mystery. This is the noble King Pelles, behind whom is that undeclared type of consecrated royalty, which was the maimed King Pellehan, whose hurt is to be healed by Galahad. The Maiden who carries the Sacred Vessel in the Pageant of the Ceremonial Rite is the Reigning King's Daughter, the *virgo intacta* Elaine. To the Castle on a certain occasion there comes the Knight Lancelot, who—as we know already—is the son of King Ban of Benoic, while his mother Helen is issued from the race of Joseph of Arimathæa, and through him is of the line of King David. It is understood by the Keeper Pelles that to bring to its final term the Mystery of the Holy Grail, his Daughter must bear a child to Lancelot, and the destined event is accomplished under circumstances of enchantment which might seem to have eliminated from the Maiden all sense of earthly passion. It cannot be said that this was the state of Lancelot, who believed that his partner in the mystery of union was the consort of Arthur the King, and to this extent the sacramental imagery offers the signs of failure. In the case of Elaine also the symbolism is stultified at a second meeting with Lancelot under almost similar circumstances. I need not specify them here, except in so far as to say that there was a plenary incursion of common motive into that which belonged otherwise to the foreordained side of things, so far as she was concerned. I can imagine nothing in the whole course of literature to compare with the original renunciation of this Maiden, on whom the pure light of the Grail had fallen for seasons and years, and who was called upon by the exigencies of the Quest to make that sacrifice which is indicated by the great Romance.[2]

The motherhood of King Pelles' Daughter, because of her consanguinity with the Mysteries, of which she is an Assistant-Guardian under the Hereditary Keeper, occurs as the result of an intercourse which has some aspects of a Magical Marriage, and, considering all its

---

[1] As the Vulgate Cycle stands in its artificial sequence, it creates an impression that the building fluctuated in the mind of Romance. We have the authority, at its value, of the GRAND SAINT GRAAL that it was *fort et bien séant* externally and a fair house within, but there is no suggestion of vast extent. Elsewhere we hear of a township within the walls; but when Lancelot pays his first visit thereto he beheld a *petit chastiel*. Sommer, *Op. cit.*, V, p. 105.

[2] At a High Festival of the Grail, when she no longer could bear the Sacred Vessel, Elaine upbraided her father who had caused her to lose that which could never be recovered. King Pelles answered that it was done for a high purpose. Sommer, *Op. cit.*, V, p. 142.

THE VULGATE CYCLE OF THE HOLY GRAIL 209

circumstances, it is difficult or impossible to speculate about all that lies behind it. We may say almost that the Lesser Mysteries took flesh for a period under an ordained enchantment and were ill at ease in their envelope. Having regard to Galahad's election, the response which he made thereto, and the achievement which in fine crowned it, the manner of his birth is no longer even a stain : it is a triviality, the sufficing cause of which removes the suggestion of profanation in respect of the Holy Place which by that unusual conception drew to the term of its ministry.[1] I can understand that the mind unversed in the harmony of the whole scheme may think that the generation of Galahad should have been left in a cloud of uncertainty and himself without declared father or mother, like the mystic King of Salem. We have to remember, however, that what we now term bastardy does not rank in the Romances as a stain of necessity upon origin : it seems almost a conventional mode of begetting heroes-in-chief, and that which obtains for Galahad obtains for the ideal Hero and King who was son according to the flesh of Uther Pendragon. As no Romances ascribe a higher importance to chastity, and even to virginity, than some of the Grail Legends, so—antecedently at least—their writers had every reason to attach its proper degree of value to the pre-eminence and sanctity of the nuptial bond ; but there was that in the antecedents and genealogy of Lancelot which made him—*ex hypothesi*—the only possible Father for a yet more exotic Flower of Chivalry, who was the predestined Grail Winner ; but at the same time nothing could insure that possibility except in the absence of his marriage.

So therefore Galahad was begotten in the fullness of time, and was seen by Sir Bors when the latter paid his first visit to Corbenic.[2] He is described as a very beautiful child of some two years old, who, according to King Pelles, would accomplish the Adventures of the Holy Grail, as testified by prophecies of saintly men. The days went on, and Bors saw Galahad again, to his great joy, when Elaine attended a great Court summoned by King Arthur at Camelot to keep the Festival of Whitsuntide.[3] The result of this visit was that Lancelot was driven forth by Guinevere and became mad through grief. In this state he reached Corbenic after a long time and was healed by the Holy Grail,[4] when he took up his abode in an island accompanied by Elaine and her suite but not apparently by Galahad, who remained at the Castle. Later on the lad expressed a wish to be near his Father and it was arranged that he should be placed in a Convent at no great distance from Camelot, where the sister of King Pelles was Abbess.[5] Meanwhile Arthur's Queen had repented or changed her mind and had summoned back Lancelot to Court. He prepared to depart, and being again at Corbenic, apparently saw his Son for the first time. Galahad subsequently was taken to the proposed Convent and there remained till

---

[1] The arrangements were made at Corbenic, but the act of intercourse took place at a Castle in the vicinity. *Op. cit.*, V, p. 109.
[2] Sommer, *Op. cit.*, V, pp. 296, 297.
[3] *Ib.*, pp. 376–380. [4] *Ib.*, p. 400. [5] *Ib.*, pp. 407, 408.

he was eighteen according to the Vulgate text, for which other manuscripts substitute fifteen or " fifteen and over ". He was seen frequently by his Father, as also by Bors and Lionel, on the witness of the Lancelot Romance, which, it must be said, does all in its power unconsciously to commonise the story of the HAUT PRINCE. It is very different with the Great Quest, which sees that a veil of concealment covers his early days. When we meet him first therein he is among the Pageants and Holy Places of Official Religion.[1] Subsequently he is taken to Court by one who seems a Steward of the Mysteries,[2] and when the Quest begins he passes at once into a world of parable and symbol, having been consecrated firstly as a Knight by his own Father, who does not seem to know him, who acts under the direction of the Stewards, while Galahad dissembles any knowledge that he might be assumed to possess. It is all as if he had come out of Hidden Places of the King. He bears the outward signs of the Mysteries and passes through Adventures as one passes through Vision : his very battles are like passages in the Spiritual Combat. The Grail of which he is in quest is more especially the Secret of High Sanctity and he moves through a realm of Masses, more sacred and more efficacious than were ever heard in Logres. He himself is the Mystery of Spiritual Chivalry exemplified in human form : his history is one of Initiation, and his term is to see God. As compared with the rest of the literature, we enter in his Legend upon new ground, and are on the eminence of Mont Salvatch rather than among the normal offices of Knighthood. It is more especially this Legend which is regarded by some scholarship as the last outcome of an ascetic element introduced into the Grail Cycle ; but it is not understood that throughout the period of the Middle Ages the mystical life manifested only under an ascetic aspect, or with an environment of that kind. The Galahad Romance is not ascetic after the ordinary way, or as the term is accepted commonly : it has an interior quality which places it above that degree, and this quality is an open sense of the mystic life. Those who have talked of asceticism meant in reality to speak of supernatural life, of which the Galahad Romance is a kind of archetypal picture. The atmosphere of the Great Quest gives up Galahad as the natural air gives up the vision from beyond. It is the story of the arch-natural man who comes to those who will receive him. He issues from the place of its Mystery, as Lancelot came from Fairyland, or at least a World of Enchantment. The atmosphere is that of Great Mysteries, the odour that of a Sanctuary withdrawn behind the Hallows of the outward Holy Places. Galahad's entire life is bound up so completely with the Quest to which he is dedicated that apart therefrom he can scarcely be said to live. The desire of a certain House not made with hands has so eaten him up that he has never entered the precincts of the halls of passion. He is indeed faithful and true ; but earthly attraction is foreign to him,

---

[1] Sommer, *Op. cit.*, VI, p. 4.
[2] *Uns preudons a une robe blanche viex et anchiens. Ib.*, p. 7.

even in its exaltation. Even his meetings with his Father are shadowy and not of this world—a characteristic which seems the more prominent when he is the better fulfilling what would be understood by his filial duty. It is not that he is explicitly outside the sphere of sense and its temptations, but that his actuating motives are of a transmuted kind. In proportion, his Quest is of the unrealised order: it is the working of a Mystery within the place of a Mystery; and it is in comparison therewith that we may understand the deep foreboding which fell upon the heart of Arthur when the flower of his wonderful Court went forth to seek the Grail. In this respect the old Legend illustrates the fact that many are called but few are chosen; and even in the latter class it is only the rarest flower of the Mystic Chivalry which can be thought of as chosen among thousands. Of the Perceval Quest—I have said—there are many versions, but of Galahad there is one story only. So are the peers of the Round Table a great company, but Galahad is one. So also, of the High Kings and Princes, there are some who come again, and of such is the Royal Arthur; but there are some who return no more, and of these is Galahad. He has not been understood even by great poets, for there could be scarcely a worse interpretation of his position than a poem, like that of Tennyson, in which he celebrates his strength on the ground that his heart is pure. Let me add, in conclusion of this part, that at the time of his coming the Grail went about in the land, looking for those it belonged to, and that in this respect Galahad had the true secret of *le moyen de parvenir*. It has its secret place of abiding, its Altar of Repose at Corbenic, the Grail Castle; but it appears at the King's Court—and this is exclusive to the story. The voice of the Quest passed through all Britain, in part by common report—because all or nearly all the Arthurian Knighthood bound itself to assume the task—but in part also by the miracle of unknown voices and of holy foreknowledge. The Grail itself is not the Official Sacrament, or it is that and something which exceeds it. If it were otherwise there would be no sense in the declaration made by a Hermit that certain Knights may seek but shall never find it. On the Eucharistic side, it is the Vision of Christ Himself, and the Mystery of Divine Providence is manifested strangely therein. It works through Faith, represented as the Way of Attainment and the Gate of Things Unseen. In the poem of Borron and other early versions, the Sacred Vessel is invisible—and that utterly—to persons of evil life; but, though still under its due veils, it is shewn in the Quest more openly, and on one occasion even to all who are present—good Knights and indifferent. The vision imposes silence, and this seems to have been always its office; but it is that kind of silence which comes about by the mode of ecstasy; and in the case of Lancelot it is described rather fully, as if there were a particular intention discernible in his advancement through those Grades of his partial Initiation, when he sees without participating. One form of this ecstasy seems to be connected with the working of the Holy Spirit. But there is no assurance to be inferred from favour to further favour, since, on another occasion, the Grail is invisible to Lancelot when it is seen at the same time and in the same place by a Company of White Knights.

Of such is the Vessel of the Legend and as regards the search after it, the Elect Knight is told that God entered into this world to free men from the Wearisome Adventures which were on them and from the evil belief. A close parallel is instituted between the Knight and Christ, since Galahad came to terminate the adventurous and evil destinies in the island of Britain. For this reason he is likened to the Son of the High Father, who brought souls out of thrall; and even a demon confesses to him as the way of truth.

I conceive that there is little occasion to recite the story of the Quest, which is available after so many manners of English vesture to young and old alike. At the Vigil of Pentecost, Lancelot was carried by a gentlewoman to a Holy House,[1] where he was required to knight the Son of his own body, but, as we have seen, without learning his name or recognising him after any manner. Galahad, who " was semely and demure as a dove, with all manner of good features," was acquainted, undoubtedly, with his geniture; but he made no claim on his Father. After this mode, at the beginning of his progress, was he consecrated by the secular order and received into the Life of Chivalry. He came forth from the sacred precincts, being a nameless convent of white nuns, wherein it is said that he had been nourished, and was brought to the Court of King Arthur by " a good old man and an ancient clothed all in white," who saluted the company at table with words of peace.[2] Against this arrival the palace had been prepared strangely by the emblazonment of letters of gold on the Siege Perilous—testifying that the time had come when it should be occupied at long last—and by the appearance of a great stone in the river outside, with a Sword embedded therein, which none present could withdraw. The ancient man uplifted the draperies of the Chair, and there was found a new emblazonment: " This is the Siege of Galahalt the High Prince." The youth is seated accordingly, as a royalty who was not of this world, and it was seen that he was clothed in red arms, though without sword or shield. But he had begun to move amidst enchantments: the sword implanted in the stone was to him predestined, and by him it was withdrawn, after which he revealed by the word of his own mouth that it was that weapon wherewith the good Knight Balyn had slain Balan, his brother. At the festival which followed this episode the Grail, under its proper veils, as I have said, appeared in the hall, illuminating all things by the grace of the Holy Ghost and imposing that sacred silence—already mentioned—which obtains in the presence of the Great Mysteries. As the light enlightened them spiritually, and to each uplifted the countenance of each in beauty, so the Sacred Vision fed them abundantly in their bodies; but because of those draperies which shrouded the Vessel,

---

[1] She came in the name of King Pelles, Keeper of the Holy Grail. Sommer, *Op cit.*, VI, Les Aventures ou la Queste del Saint Graal, p. 1.

[2] Also he announced Galahad as the " desired Knight," of King David's high lineage, who was to achieve the Adventures of Logres and of realms beyond. *Op. cit.*, p. 7.

THE VULGATE CYCLE OF THE HOLY GRAIL 213

the Great Chivalry vowed to go in quest thereof, that they might see it more openly. After this manner began the fateful inquisition which, by a messenger from Nasciens the Second—who was the early Keeper of Galahad according to the VULGATE MERLIN—was forbidden to natural women, like that of Masonry, though the ministers of the Grail were Maidens.

The first adventures of Galahad were those which befell him at an Abbey of white monks, when he who was as yet without a shield received that which Joseph II gave in the far past to Evalach, that he might prevail against the King of Egypt—that also which Joseph crossed with his blood on his death-bed. It was a sign that the Evil Adventures would be ended by Galahad. Previously, it had been a shield perilous to all who used it, because it was predestined to one; but I do not find that it has a special office in the later part of the Legend.

Of the Grail and the other Hallows, of their Ministry and Mystery, and of all things connected therewith, we have heard in their proper sections otherwise. After what manner Lancelot, Perceval and Bors passed through Worlds of Parable—as through places of purification—I do not speak here, and even in respect of the High Prince, I am concerned only in so far as his story completes the things which were left over from other branches of the Vulgate Chronicles: the healing of Mordrains, the King-Penitent of all the centuries; the release of Simeon;[1] and the manumission of the unfaithful Moses. But of this last I find nothing in the Quest. As regards Simeon, the Abbey which was visited by Lancelot was reached by Galahad towards the close of his time of Quest, and there he beheld a burning wood in a croft under the Minster. But the "flaming failed, and the fire staunched" as he drew thereto, and so paused for a space. The voice of Simeon from within greeted him in a good hour, when Galahad was to draw a soul out of earthly pain into joy of Paradise. It said also that he who spoke was of his kindred, and that for three hundred and fifty-four years he had been purged thus of the sin which he had done against Joseph of Arimathæa—or rather not against him but the High Office of the Grail. Galahad took the body in his arms, bore it into the Minster, had service said over it, and interred it before the High Altar. Of such was the rest of Simeon.

It was at another Abbey that he came upon the age-long vigil of King Mordrains.[2] Galahad had hands of healing, and seeing that he was born in the Sanctuary, it may be said that in this Romance the healing comes from within. These were the words of the King: "Galahad the servant of Jesus Christ whose coming I have awaited so long, now embrace me and let me rest on thy breast, so that I may rest between thine arms, for thou art a clean virgin above all Knights as the flower of the lily, in whom virginity is signified, and thou art the rose the which is the flower of all good virtues, and in colour of fire. For the fire of the Holy Ghost is taken so in thee that my flesh which was of dead oldness,

[1] *Op. cit.*, p. 186. [2] *Op. cit.*, pp. 184, 185.

is become young again." When Galahad heard his words, he covered his whole body in a close embrace, in which position the King prays Christ to visit him, wherein and whereafter the soul departed from his body. So was the curious impertinent, who had been called but not chosen at that time, after his long penance, at length forgiven the offence, and was taken into the great peace, fortified with all Rites of the Most Secret and Holy Church of the Hidden Grail.

The Ship of Solomon had, prior to these episodes, conveyed the Questing Knights—Galahad, Perceval and Bors—from point to point in their progress;[1] it had taken Lancelot a certain distance in his Son's company, till they commended each other to God for the rest of their mortal life; it had borne the Sister of Perceval, who of her own hair and of silk, combined with precious stones, had braided the true and proper girdle for the Sword of David, to replace the mean girdle attached to it by the wife of Solomon. But she had yielded her life before Mordrains had passed in God, and her body had been placed by her proper desire in another ship, with a covenant on her part that it should meet the Questers at Sarras, when the Ship of Solomon brought them to that bourne of their voyaging. It remained only that those three should now gather at Corbenic for the healing of the maimed King Pellinor or Pellehan, about whose place and identity we have seen that the text offers some elements of minor confusion. This is he whom we must suppose to have received the Dolorous Stroke at the hands of Balyn.

As the Path of Quest drew towards its central point, the three, who had traversed various converging roads, met, as it is said, at travers, knowing that the Adventures of Logres were at last achieved. They entered the Castle, and King Pelles greeted them with great joy.[2] In this as in some other Romances grave importance is attached to resoldering the Broken Sword, and that which was brought by Eleazer, the King's son, was that with which Joseph II was once stricken through the thighs. It was set perfectly by Galahad when the others had essayed in vain, and was then given to Bors, as a good Knight and a worthy man. What followed thereon was the sustenance of the elect Grail Knights after a spiritual manner, to the exclusion of the general assembly, who were dismissed from the presence. Those who remained were three and three, namely, Galahad, Perceval and Bors, for the first triad; for the second, King Pelles, his son Eleazar, and a Maiden who was the King's niece, as also the Grail Bearer in succession to Elaine after the conception of Galahad. To these were joined certain pilgrims who were Knights also, namely, three of Gaul, three of Ireland, and three of Denmark. Finally, there was brought in the Maimed King, and thereon a voice said that two of those who were present did not belong to the Quest, at which words King Pelles—although he was the

[1] It is said in one place that Galahad and Perceval were together for five years, during which they achieved The Adventures of Logres; but these are not recounted.
[2] Sommer, *Op. cit.*, VI, pp. 187 *et seq.*

THE VULGATE CYCLE OF THE HOLY GRAIL 215

Keeper—rose up with his son and departed. They were therefore thirteen in all; and according to the text of Malory, one of these was a woman, who was present with them when Joseph II, the first Bishop of Christendom, came down with Angels from Heaven, and celebrated an Arch-Natural Mass in the Holy Place. After the Kiss of Peace given to Galahad, and communicated by him to his fellows, the Celebrants dissolved; but out of the Grail itself there came the Saviour of all, with the signs of His passion upon Him, and communicated to them all in the Eucharist. He also vanished, and Galahad, who had received his instructions, went up to the maimed King and anointed him with the Blood flowing from the Hallowed Spear. Thereupon, he, being healed, rose up and gave thanks to God. It is said that, in the sequel of time, he united himself to a company of white monks.[1]

"Sir," said Galahad to the Great Master at the close of the Mysteries, "why shall not these other fellows go with us?"—that is to say, unto Sarras, the reference being to the Nine Mysterious Knights. The answer hereto was significant: "For this cause: for right as I departed my apostles, one here and another there, so I will that ye depart, and two of you shall die in my service, but one of you shall come again and tell tidings." So, therefore, the Company of Adepts dissevered; but we have seen how Galahad, Perceval and Bors were carried by the Ship of Solomon to Sarras, "in the parts of Babylon," called an island in the Quest. There met them, in accordance with her covenant, that other barque, which bore the body of Perceval's most holy Sister. We have seen also how the soul of Galahad departed, and it rests only to say that Perceval died in a hermitage; but Sir Bors returned to Logres, bearing the messages of his brethren, especially of Galahad to his Father: "And when he had said these words Galahad went to Perceval and kissed him and commended him to God, and so he went to Sir Bors, and kissed him, and commended him to God, and said: "Fair Lord, salute me to my Lord Sir Lancelot, my Father. And as soon as you see him, bid him remember of this unstable world."

The bodies of Perceval and Galahad were buried in the spiritualities of Sarras, which may have been in some sense a City of Initiation, though until their coming it was ruled by evil rather than good. It was not the abiding place, but that of the final trial for the Stewards of the Mystery, and at first they were imprisoned therein; though Galahad was afterwards made King. The Spear was taken into Heaven, together with the Holy Vessel, but Bors returned—as it has been intimated—carrying the resoldered Broken Sword, as if grace had been removed, but not that which now may have symbolised the coming destruction of the Round Table. Of the Sword of David we hear nothing further, nor do we know what became of the Ship of Solomon. As the symbol of Faith, it may have continued voyaging; but on other considerations it had done its work: there was perhaps no reason why it should remain when Galahad had gone.

[1] *Op. cit.*, p. 191.

Perhaps the saddest mystery of all is the end of King Pelles himself, and how it fared with him after the departure of the Grail. It will be seen that the Quest versions offer many alternatives, but there is one text only which says that the Hereditary Keeper was dispossessed utterly and left in an empty Sanctuary.

VIII

THE WELSH QUEST OF GALAHAD

IT is considered that this translation, the only manuscript of which is referable to the early part of the fifteenth century,[1] was (1) made from another codex than that which was used by Malory for the MORTE D'ARTHUR or by Furnivall for the Roxburghe Club; (2) that it is the transcript of an earlier copy; (3) that the Welsh rendering was the work of Siencyn ab John, who is said to have flourished three centuries before Caxton. As this date is mythical, we may be content to note (1) that the French original—like other QUESTE texts—embodied material from the GRAND SAINT GRAAL; (2) that outside all evidences of mistranslation, the WELSH QUEST differs in several particulars from codices which are known to scholarship, while (3) it seems fairly probable that the variations are not those of invention. On the one hand, there is a slight but not inappreciable attenuation of the mystical atmosphere with which we are lovingly familiar in the old Caxton text, though the general features remain: for example, the strange enhanced knowledge of one another which is attributed in the Malory version to the Knights who beheld the Holy Vessel, under the veils thereof, at the King's Table, is wanting in the Welsh version.[2] Alternatively, there are other respects in which there is an added disposition to dwell on the spiritual side of things found in the French source, and this is manifested plainly in a few crucial cases. The Table of the Lord's Supper is described as that which fed the body and the soul with Heavenly Food, while the Grail itself is said to provide a Spiritual nourishment, which is sent by the Holy Ghost to him who seeks in Grace to sit at the Table thereof.[3] The intimate connection between the Sacred Vessel and the Office of the Divine Spirit—which is so evident in the Metrical Romance of Borron—is apparent also, and one who is on the Quest is told that by falling into sin he will fail to see that Spirit, even as Lancelot failed.[4] Outside those rare wanderings of the Holy

---

[1] Y SAINT GREAL, edited by the Rev. Robert Williams, being Vol. I of the Hengwrt MSS., 1876.

[2] MORTE DARTHUR, Book XIII, cap. 5. Cf., however, LA QUESTE, Sommer, Op. cit., VI, p. 13. It is Malory who enhances the atmosphere.

[3] Hengwrt MSS., I, p. 495. The wording is vague and elusive: (1) "The Holy Spirit will send," (2) "to him that seeks by Grace," (3) "to sit at the Table of the Holy Grail". It suggests almost an inward experience, as if the Grail comes to a seeker who follows its Quest within. Cf. LA QUESTE, same edition, p. 113, omitted in Malory's abbreviated version.

[4] Hengwrt MSS., p. 470. The words are: "Thou wilt fail to see the Holy Ghost," referring to the Blessed Vessel. It follows that he who sees the Grail sees also the Holy Spirit. Cf. the QUESTE, Op. cit., p. 58, which speaks only of failure in the Quest.

THE VULGATE CYCLE OF THE HOLY GRAIL 217

Grail which are recorded in the French text, there are vague, aloof references to its manifestation at sundry places in Logres—or there more especially, if not there to the exclusion of other regions. Finally as to this part, I recognise an added atmosphere of suggested Mystery as regards the House of the Hallows.[1] This was the permanent Shrine of the Holy Vessel; but whether the latter was visible always to those who dwelt within, or only at certain times and seasons, is not clear from any extant text: it remains indeed doubtful on the evidence of all the French Cycle. Hence it is open to question whether it was the daily nourishment of the House, or whether its varied ministry was contingent on the arrival of a stranger who was prepared so far sufficiently that he was admitted within the gates. It was the latter probably, because Lancelot abode in the House for four days; but it was not until the fifth day, and then in the midst of a supper, that the Grail appeared and filled all with the meats most loved by them.

The Welsh Quest, like its prototype of Northern France, draws—as already noted—from the GRAND SAINT GRAAL, but not always from one of those codices with which we have been made acquainted so far by the pains of scholarship. For example, the account of the Second Table is given with specific variations, though there is nothing to justify their enumeration in this place, except that the Son of Joseph is said to have occupied the Seat which corresponded to that of Christ, and no one ventured to take it after him. It was not so occupied in the parent historical text; and we know, of course, that the Siege Perilous in other presentations of the Legend is that of Judas Iscariot.

What appears to be regarded as the Dolorous Stroke in the WELSH QUEST misreads the same source as follows: (1) King Lambor was father of the Lame King, and was at war with King Urlain, formerly a Saracen. (2) Lambor was forced to flight, followed by his pursuer, and in doing so reached the seashore, where he found the Ship of Solomon. (3) He took up the Sword therein and smote Urlain, so that he and his horse were cut in two pieces. This occurred in England, and was the first blow that was ever given with the weapon. (4) The King who was slain is said to have been so holy that great vengeance was taken by God for that blow. (5) In neither kingdom—meaning those of the two combatants—was there found any fruit for a long time, everything being dried up, so that the territories are called to this day the Decayed Kingdom. It is to be observed that this is in direct contradiction to the particulars in the GRAND SAINT GRAAL concerning the death of Lambor, who was Keeper at that time of the Sacred Vessel.[2] The story of Balyn and Balan was of course unknown to the Welsh translator.

As regards the Lame or Maimed King, he was an Uncle of Perceval,

[1] It must not be supposed that the Welsh version presents new things, in the order of episodes or otherwise. It has a certain manner of treatment which leads me to dwell briefly upon a few points which have been passed over or barely cited in my account of the Vulgate QUESTE.

[2] It is in equal contradiction as regards the French QUESTE itself. Cf. Sommer, *Op. cit.*, VI, pp. 146, 147. Cf. Malory, Book XVII, cap. 3. Urlain was a newly converted "Saracen" and the "holy" King was Lambor.

and so good was his manner of living that his like could not be found in the world. One day he was hunting, and came to the seashore, where he also found the Ship of Solomon. In spite of the warning written therein, he entered without fear, and drew the Sword partly from the scabbard. He was struck by a spear in the thighs, and was maimed from that time forward. In the French QUEST OF GALAHAD this episode is attributed to Pellinor.[1]

As an illustration of general intention prevailing through the Welsh Quest, and reflected from the French text, a hermit reminds Gawain that the dignity of Knighthood was conferred upon him—among other things—for the defence of the Church,[2] and as this specific statement is part only of the general atmosphere through which the Romance moves, it will be for most an eloquent commentary on the alleged underlying hostility to official ecclesiasticism which is sometimes traced in the literature, though it is conceivable that others may be asking which Church is intended. In any case, the condition of Wales at the time of the Quest, as it is depicted in the Welsh text, is not an encouraging report regarding the last stronghold of the Celtic Church; but it is possible that the worst particulars are things which the translator has interpolated.

Whether in their agreement or variation, the details of the story do not call to be scheduled here; but there are a few points which may be noted with all brevity. Galahad is introduced at the Court of King Arthur, not alone as the desired Knight descended from David and Joseph of Arimathæa but as one on whom rest all the Adventures and Wonders of Great Britain and all countries.[3] He is called the Son of the Daughter of King Pelles; but the later story speaks invariably of the Grail Castle as that of King Peleur, whom I should identify—*sub nomine* Pellehan—as the maimed and abdicated Keeper who was healed by Galahad in the French version, of which, however, there is no mention in the Welsh Quest. The manifested Festival of the Grail in the hall of Arthur is heralded by an unknown messenger—a " gentle and fair young Maiden " on a white palfrey, who gives warning concerning its advent, and this is found also in Malory's version. So great are the delicacies at the table, by the provision of the Sacred Vessel, so much are they dwelt on in the Welsh version, that the resolution of the Knights in respect of the coming Quest has the aspect of material appetite: they resolve not to rest till they can eat at another table where they will be fed as rarely. According to Gawain, there is no such place on earth, except the Court of King Peleur. When the Quest is thus undertaken Galahad says nothing. All this is an accident of aspect; for elsewhere it is stated (1) that no one shall see the Holy Grail except through the gate which is called Confession, and this is obviously the gate of the Eucharist; (2) that the final return of Bors

---

[1] To Pelles, in the version of Malory; but when the Quest ends at Corbenic Pelles is whole and sound. However, there is another maimed King, who is not named in the story, but is obviously Pellehan.

[2] Sommer, *Op. cit.*, VI, p. 39.   [3] *Ib.*, pp. 7, 8.

was designed to exhibit the spirituality of that good which at the last end of things was lost by so many on account of their sins.

The time comes when Galahad swears upon the Relics with the others to maintain the Quest, and, apart from this position—which has not been understood by scholarship—there are episodes and intimations which seem intended to shew that the natural child of the Sanctuary was not permitted to know all—though he had that which was implied in his heirship—until, in common with the others, he undertook the great enterprise. The Knights proceeded on their journey weeping and in great sorrow—that is to say, with failing hearts, foreboding the discounselling of so many and all the disaster coming after: *Euntes ibant et flebant.*

There is one reference to Eleazar, the son of King Pelles, and one to a Knight named Argus, who, by an unthinkable confusion, is said to be the son of Elaine, as if this Daughter of the House had married or begotten subsequently. The Hermit, Nasciens II, whose identity is so important for the GRAND SAINT GRAAL, is misdescribed as the son-in-law of Evalach, no extant text disclosing that he in fact is the witness of its PROLOGUE, except the HUTH MERLIN. He is found on one occasion by Gawain in a very poor cell or hermitage, with a small chapel attached.

When the Questing Knights arrive at the Grail Castle, it is not said that they see either Pelles or Peleur, nor are these or Eleazar present at the manifestation of the Holy Grail. The Maiden who remains in the text of Malory is bidden also to depart, following in this respect the chief French manuscripts. He who comes down from Heaven as the first Bishop of Christendom is distinguished rightly from Joseph of Arimathæa, and is therefore the Second Joseph. When he celebrates the Secret Mass of the Grail, he takes out a wafer from the Vessel, which shews that it was used as a Ciborium. In the Divine Discourse thereafter, it is said by Christ that many a good man has come to the Castle through the Grace of the Holy Ghost. As regards the nine mysterious Knights who are not to accompany the three on their journey to Sarras, the parting of those with these takes place amidst great brotherhood, and each of them says who he is; but the nine are not named in the text. Galahad asks them to salute Arthur if they go to his Court, and they reply that they shall do so gladly; but they do not say that they will go. Probably they went back by another way into their own countries.

Now, these are the chief points which I proposed to set forth; and there is one thing more only—that the Spear was not taken to Sarras, nor was it removed to Heaven with the Sacred Vessel. In conclusion as to the QUEST OF GALAHAD, the presence of that Maiden who was niece of King Pelles at the great vision of the Grail seems without authority in extant French texts: it is therefore peculiar to Malory and the version which he followed.

This is the end of this publication.

Any remaining blank pages are for our book binding requirements and are blank on purpose.

To search thousands of interesting publications like this one, please remember to visit our website at:

http://www.kessinger.net

CPSIA information can be obtained at www.ICGtesting.com
Printed in the USA
LVOW09*1629131114

413209LV00017BA/86/P